Every Vote Counts

A PRACTICAL GUIDE TO CHOOSING THE NEXT PRESIDENT

Chris Katsaropoulos

800 East 96th Street, Indianapolis, Indiana 46240

Every Vote Counts: A Practical Guide to Choosing the Next President

International Standard Book Number: 0-7897-3284-X

Library of Congress Catalog Card Number: 2004106818

Printed in the United States of America

First Printing: August 2004

06 05 04 4 3 2 1

Trademarks

Warning and Disclaimer

Bulk Sales

Que Publishing offers excellent discounts on this book when ordered in quantity for bulk purchases or special sales. For more information, please contact:

U.S. Corporate and Government Sales
1-800-382-3419
corpsales@pearsontechgroup.com

For sales outside of the U.S., please contact:

International Sales
+1-317-581-3793
international@pearsontechgroup.com

Publisher
Paul Boger

Development Editor
Laura Norman

Technical Editor
Erik Hromadka

Managing Editor
Charlotte Clapp

Project Editor
Andy Beaster

Copy Editor
Margo Catts

Indexer
Ken Johnson

Proofreader
Mike Henry

Publishing Coordinator
Cindy Teeter

Interior Designer
Sandra Schroeder

Cover Designer
Sandra Schroeder

Page Layout
Brad Chinn

Contents at a Glance

Table of Contents

About the Author

Chris Katsaropoulos is author of more than a dozen computer trade books and text books, including the bestsellers *Learning to Create a Web Page with Microsoft Office* and *Learning the Internet for Business.* Chris has worked as editor and product manager for major trade and textbook companies, including Pearson Education (formerly Macmillan Computer Publishing), Glencoe/McGraw-Hill, Thomson/Course Technology, DDC Publishing, and Scott, Foresman. Chris is a non-partisan observer of politics who shares the viewpoint and chief concern of independent and undecided voters everywhere: How can I choose the best candidate for president in 2004?

Dedication

To Tracy, Katie, and Alex.

Acknowledgments

My sincere thanks to Paul Boger for giving me the opportunity to write this book and the input to make it better. Also, thanks to my editors at Pearson: development editor Laura Norman, technical editor Erik Hromadka, copy editor Margo Catts, and project editor Andy Beaster for their insightful comments and quick work on a very tight deadline.

Tell Us What You Think!

As the reader of this book, *you* are our most important critic and commentator. We value your opinion and want to know what we're doing right, what we could do better, what areas you'd like to see us publish in, and any other words of wisdom you're willing to pass our way.

You can email or write me directly to let me know what you did or didn't like about this book—as well as what we can do to make our books stronger.

When you write, please be sure to include this book's title and author as well as your name and phone or email address. I will carefully review your comments and share them with the author and editors who worked on the book.

Email: feedback@quepublishing.com

Mail: Paul Boger
Publisher
Que/Sams Publishing
800 East 96th Street
Indianapolis, IN 46240 USA

Reader Services

For more information about this book or others from Que Publishing, visit our Web site at **www.quepublishing.com**. Type the ISBN (excluding hyphens) or the title of the book in the Search box to find the book you're looking for.

Introduction

What's This Book All About?

By all accounts, the 2004 presidential election is shaping up to be one of the closest in history. Polls show that the candidates have been neck and neck for months and the alignment of states leaning towards Bush or Kerry is similar to the breakdown of states voting for Bush and Gore in 2000.

This year's tight race and the aftermath of the 2000 election, in which a few thousand votes decided the outcome, means *every vote counts.* If you're undecided or confused—if the election-year rhetoric makes you want to turn off the TV or change the channel—this book is designed for you.

Every Vote Counts is a practical guide to the three major presidential candidates—Bush, Kerry, Nader—and their campaign strategies and tactics. It's a brief but comprehensive guide to where the candidates stand on all the key issues and what drives them to take those positions.

The book includes a Comparison Guide that helps you weigh the candidates' positions on key issues side by side, as well as a Candidate Match Survey you can take to see how your views stack up to those of the candidates.

Every Vote Counts is also a guide that helps you cut through the campaign rhetoric and public relations strategies designed to deceive and distract you from making a thoughtful choice when you head to the polls in November.

In Part I, "Understanding the Campaign," you get a quick, insightful overview of how the candidates craft their messages to you, how they run their campaigns, and how they try to swing you into their camp. You'll find out how Bush and Kerry use negative TV ads, high-tech polling, campaign fund raising, and savvy public relations to sell themselves to you.

Learning these tricks of the trade will help you decipher the true meanings behind the media messages and make a much more informed decision about who's the right candidate for you.

The book's many sidebars help you learn how rapidly shifting current events can impact the election and help you evaluate how Bush, Kerry, and Nader would respond to these complex issues. You can also go online to the book's web site (**www.quepublishing.com/everyvotecounts/**) to learn more about how these issues change as you use the book.

You'll also learn about the character issues—leadership, integrity, and personality—that often tip the scales for undecided voters in a close race.

In Part II, "Comparing the Candidates," you get the Candidate Comparison Guide and the Candidate Match Survey, as well as a complete chapter on each candidate that gives an in-depth look at their positions on the issues and the key life and career events that made them who they are today.

You also get a final chapter on how to make sure your vote counts on election day, including a summary of voter registration requirements in all 50 states, and a list of your rights as a voter at the polls.

Even if you already know who you want to vote for this fall, *Every Vote Counts* will help you learn more about the candidates and where they stand on the issues. It's the perfect guide to make sure you can be an informed and active voter in this important election.

I

Understanding the Campaign

1

"America will never be destroyed from the outside. If we falter and lose our freedoms, it will be because we destroyed ourselves."

—Abraham Lincoln

Every Vote Counts: The Electoral College, Hanging Chads, and Why Your Vote Matters

269 votes. That's all it takes to change the course of history in America.

In 2000, more than 186 million people were eligible to vote for president. Of those, only 130 million people were registered. And only 105 million of the people who could have voted for president actually did.

25 million people sat on the sidelines in 2000 when they could have made a difference—one way or the other—in an election where a swing of only 269 votes would have changed the outcome of the election. More people show up for a typical high school basketball game or the afternoon screening of a B movie at the multiplex.

Democracy, Hanging by a Chad

The 269 votes we're talking about here are the number of votes Al Gore needed to carry Florida and win the state's 25 electoral votes—25 votes that would have put him over the national majority required to win a presidential election.

We all remember the disputed election in 2000—the frenzied TV news reports describing behind-the-scenes legal wrangling, the confusion over so-called "butterfly ballots," the protest marches, lawsuits, "hanging chads," and, ultimately, the decision handed down by the U.S. Supreme Court in the landmark case of *Bush v. Gore* that decided the election.

Only 50.6% of the people in Florida who were *eligible* to vote in 2000 actually made the effort to cast a ballot—that is just over half. The rest of the people were busy doing something else that day, when they could have made a difference one way or the other.

Let's face it—we're all part of the problem to some extent. How many of us can honestly say we've voted in every primary, for every "meaningless" local office in every off-year election? Voter turnout in presidential elections has declined from 63% to around 50% since 1960 when John F. Kennedy squeaked into office. In years when we're not voting for president, participation dips as low as 36% (see Table 1.1).

Democracy is not guaranteed. It's not so much a right or a privilege as an act, something we create as we go. It requires participation to function as advertised.

The Constitution and the various electoral procedures upon which our government is based provide the legal framework for democracy. What we choose to do with it from there is strictly up to us. Choosing a truly representative government—in this case, a president who represents the will of the people—depends on maximum participation.

Table 1.1 National Voter Turnout in Presidential Elections: 1960–2000

Year	Voting Age Population	Registration	Turnout	% T/O of Voting Age Population
2000	205,815,000	156,421,311	105,586,274	51.3%
1996	196,511,000	146,211,960	96,456,345	49.1%
1992	189,529,000	133,821,178	104,405,155	55.1%
1988	182,778,000	126,379,628	91,594,693	50.1%
1984	174,466,000	124,150,614	92,652,680	53.1%
1980	164,597,000	113,043,734	86,515,221	52.6%
1976	152,309,000	105,037,986	81,555,221	53.6%
1972	140,776,000	97,328,541	77,718,554	55.2%
1968	120,328,000	81,658,180	73,211,875	60.8%
1964	114,090,000	73,715,818	70,644,592	61.9%
1960	109,159,000	64,833,096	68,838,204	63.1%

Source: Federal Election Commission

LOW-HANGING CHADS

Whatever happened to those hanging chads, the little shreds of paper that dangled from Florida's disputed punchcard ballots in the 2000 election? After all the problems with the punchcard voting system and other antiquated methods used in Florida and elsewhere, have we done anything about it?

Well, yes and no. Many voting districts across the country have taken the initiative to replace the older systems with new technology. But there are concerns about implementing the new systems.

Several of Florida's largest counties, including Palm Beach, Broward, and Miami-Dade—site of some of the most contentious chad disputes in 2000—made the switch to new systems in time for the 2002 election.

Judging from the problems encountered with the new computerized voting machines, we might be better off going back to the chads. Problems with the new machines ranged from votes lost because of improper shutdown of the machines to machines that simply did not work.

In one precinct with more than 1,000 eligible voters, no votes were recorded, although it's hard to believe no one showed up. In one election with a margin of victory of 12 votes, the computerized machines recorded 130 so-called "non-votes," in which people supposedly showed up to cast a ballot with no choice.

Some machines froze while voters cast their votes. In Maryland, software glitches caused machines in 30 precincts to identify all voters as Democrats. There is also concern about the possibility that hackers or partisan operatives could easily manipulate the electronic election results—either in "real-time" on site at a precinct or remotely via an Internet connection to the databases of results maintained by the voting machine companies.

The range of technical problems makes the antiquated Election 2000 punch card follies seem like a kinder, gentler Y2K bug. Perhaps the most troubling problem encountered with the new machines is the fact that a recount is not possible with the new systems because there is no paper record of each vote...

Photo by Robert King/Newsmakers.

Florida election official inspects a punchcard ballot for signs of dimpling.

Why Bother? Voter Apathy and Its Causes

It's not hard to pinpoint the reasons behind voter apathy. Participation in all sorts of civic organizations and activities is down, from bowling leagues to Rotary clubs to political parties. Our time is consumed by individual pursuits—longer work hours, more entertainment options, more technological ways to "stay connected"—cell phones, email, instant messaging—than gathering at the local Moose Lodge.

At the same time, the advent of squawk box pundits on TV, on radio, and in books has created a climate in which politics has become more polarized and shrill—a turnoff to many who might otherwise be engaged in a discussion of the issues.

Undecided and Unimpressed

All this bickering may be fine for the party faithful, dyed-in-the-wool Republicans or Democrats, who identify strongly with the traditional conservative or liberal positions attached to the parties. But America has become more complex in the post-industrial age, an era in which whole sectors of the economy can experience upheaval in a matter of months, demographic change is happening faster than ever before, and our foreign relations are troubled by hidden and ever-shifting enemies.

You may be one of the millions of Americans who are looking to candidates for creative solutions to these complex issues. We seek more practical approaches to solving the problems we face—solutions that don't necessarily fit within the party lines, beholden to special interests such as big oil, trial lawyers, and teachers unions.

Undecided or non-partisan voters may be just as passionate about the issues and what's at stake as party loyalists. For example, an independent, non-partisan voter (let's call her Janet) might have strong opinions about protecting the environment, allowing same-sex marriage, and keeping taxes low.

In political shorthand, Janet is liberal on social issues and conservative on economic issues—not a good fit with the positions staked out by either of the major parties. She's likely to view the election as a choice between the lesser of two evils. If none of the candidates are appealing, she may be more likely not to vote than a party member.

There's a growing category of voters like Janet—intelligent, creative, and willing to support a candidate who can respond to their subtle and non-partisan opinions. This book was written to help people like her—undecided, independent, but very interested in the outcome of the election—choose the best candidate.

★ *WHAT HE SAYS:*
"States should have the right to enact reasonable laws and restrictions particularly to end the inhumane practice of ending a life that otherwise could live."
—George W. Bush

★ *WHAT HE WANTS YOU TO HEAR:*
I'm opposed to abortion.

★ *BUT DON'T FORGET...*
Bush supports the death penalty and executed 152 people during his two terms as governor of Texas.

We Know What We Want

If you do have a strong party allegiance, this book can help you too. It can help you understand the process behind the presidential campaign and the detailed positions behind the message of each candidate. Even if you've already decided which candidate you like—be it Bush, Kerry, or Nader—this book provides a wealth of information about your favorite and how he stacks up against his opponents.

By taking the in-depth Candidate Match Survey in Chapter 12, you can see how closely your views fit with the platforms of each candidate. Who knows—you may be surprised to find that you have more in common with one of the other candidates than you expected. At the very least, the survey will help you get a comprehensive picture of how your own views tie in with the parties and their candidates. And the more informed you are as a voter, the more likely you are to get out and vote.

Find out how you can register to vote in your state by turning to Chapter 13, "The Bottom Line: Casting Your Vote," **p. 199**.

One Measly Vote

Perhaps the biggest cause of voter apathy in America is the feeling that one measly vote can't possibly matter in a nationwide election in which millions of votes are cast. Perhaps you're feeling this way too. This attitude is due to a number of factors, including

- ✓ Media coverage that treats the campaign like a horse race, focusing on momentum, who's in the lead, and predicting a winner instead of focusing on the issues
- ✓ The growing influence of high-dollar campaign contributors and special interests
- ✓ The belief that the Electoral College means my vote does not matter in presidential elections

All these views are certainly based in a measure of reality.

The way our campaigns are covered by the media does indeed have a dampening effect on voter turnout—especially when TV networks predict the winner of an election hours before the voting booths close.

But you can combat this intrusive practice by following the advice in the first part of the old saying: "Vote early and often." Going to the polls first thing in the morning, before you go to work, ensures that your vote will be among the ones that influence the media projections.

Special interests and big-bucks contributors do have a heavy impact on the platforms and positions the candidates choose. Newspaper reports about the size of a candidate's "war chest" help play up the momentum factor in the campaign horse race—especially during the primaries. Stories about a candidate's lack of funding can become a self-fulfilling prophecy—a sign that Candidate X is less popular and losing the race.

But every single one of us is entitled to only one vote—no matter how much money we have. And all the money in the candidates' war chests is only used to get out the message and *influence how you vote.* In the end, it's the ballot you cast that makes the difference.

CAN IT HAPPEN AGAIN?
George W. Bush wasn't the first president to be elected with fewer popular votes than the opposing candidate. John Quincy Adams, Rutherford B. Hayes, and Benjamin Harrison all received fewer popular votes than their opponents but still wound up in the Oval Office because they earned more electoral votes. Polls show Bush and Kerry running neck and neck—just as close as Bush and Gore were in 2000. Will the Electoral College vote differ from the popular vote again this year?

Graduating from the Electoral College

If the Florida 2000 debacle accomplished anything, it made a lot more people aware of what the Electoral College is and how it works. Before November 2000, many people assumed they had a direct vote for the president.

The problems in Florida brought the strengths *and* weaknesses of the Electoral College system to the forefront. The trials and tribulations of Election 2000 made us realize that every vote *does* count, even in a system such as the Electoral College in which our votes only serve to determine a winner-take-all slate of electors from each state.

HOW YOUR VOTE BECOMES AN ELECTORAL VOTE

The founding fathers designed the Electoral College system as a compromise to balance the interests of smaller states versus larger states and to shield the presidential election from the vagaries of a popular vote. Bottom line, they didn't really trust the common citizen to decide who the president should be, so they created the buffer of the Electoral College.

Here's how your vote for president gets translated into an Electoral College vote:

- ✓ The number of Electoral College votes your state receives is determined by the number of Senators from your state (always 2) plus the number of U.S. Representatives from your state. For example, Indiana has 11 Electoral College votes—2 Senators plus 9

Representatives. The minimum number a state can have is 3—2 Senators and 1 Representative. See Table 1.2 for a breakdown of electoral votes by state.

- ✓ The political parties in your state select a group—or slate—of electors pledged to their respective candidates. In Indiana, for example, the parties select 11 electors—equal to the number of Electoral College votes.
- ✓ On election day in November, you cast your vote for the party slate of electors representing your choice for president. Your ballot will typically say "Electors for... Bush" or "Electors for... Kerry." You're voting for the slate of electors—not the candidate himself.
- ✓ If your party wins the popular vote in your state, then the party's slate of electors becomes your state's slate of electors. If your party loses the popular vote in your state, your party sends no electors to the Electoral College from your state. Because you're voting for slates of electors, it's a winner-take-all affair.
- ✓ On the Monday following the second Wednesday in December (that's the way the law states it), the electors from each state meet in their respective state capitols and cast their electoral votes. Each elector casts one vote for president and one vote for vice president. This December date is one reason why many were pressing to have the Florida 2000 vote recounts finished so soon after the election.
- ✓ On January 6, the President of the Senate opens and reads the sealed Electoral College votes in front of the full Congress.
- ✓ The presidential candidate who receives an absolute majority of Electoral College votes—one more than half of the total—wins the election. The vice presidential candidate must also win by an absolute majority. There are currently 538 electors, or votes, in the Electoral College. 270 is the magic number of votes candidates must achieve to be elected (one more than half, which is 269).
- ✓ If no candidate achieves an absolute majority of votes, the presidential election is kicked to the House of Representatives, where each state casts one vote for one of the top three candidates.

Again, an absolute majority of votes is required to win. The Senate uses the same process to pick the vice president if none of the vice presidential candidates achieves a majority of electoral votes. The election was thrown to the House in 1801, when it required 36 House votes to select Thomas Jefferson over Aaron Burr—a *vice presidential* candidate.

- ✓ The newly elected president is sworn into office at noon on January 20.

Table 1.2 Electoral College Votes

State	Votes	State	Votes
Alabama	9	Illinois	21
Alaska	3	Indiana	11
Arizona	10	Iowa	7
Arkansas	6	Kansas	6
California	55	Kentucky	8
Colorado	9	Louisiana	9
Connecticut	7	Maryland	10
Delaware	3	Massachusetts	12
District of Columbia	3	Michigan	17
Florida	27	Minnesota	10
Georgia	15	Mississippi	6
Hawaii	4	Missouri	11
Idaho	4	Montana	3

Table 1.2 Continued

State	Votes	State	Votes
Nevada	5	South Carolina	8
New Hampshire	4	South Dakota	3
New Jersey	15	Tennessee	11
New Mexico	5	Texas	34
New York	31	Utah	5
North Carolina	15	Vermont	3
North Dakota	3	Virginia	13
Ohio	20	Washington	11
Oklahoma	7	West Virginia	5
Oregon	7	Wisconsin	10
Pennsylania	21	Wyoming	3
Rhode Island	4		

Why do we put up with a system that seems so fraught with problems? Well, despite the uproar after 2000, there are some clear advantages to the Electoral College. The system prevents a regional candidate from being elected by winning a substantial popular vote majority in one part of the country.

Candidates are forced to run on a broad range of issues to gather support from different constituencies. Without the Electoral College system, candidates could focus their efforts on large metropolitan areas such as New York and ignore the needs of rural voters. Because candidates have to win state by state, the election process becomes more of a grass-roots effort and increases the involvement of state parties in the national election.

Still, there are some definite downsides. The most glaring weakness is the fact that individual votes in smaller states are more valuable than those from larger states. Electoral College votes are allocated to each state based on the number of members of Congress each state has.

Small states such as Vermont or South Dakota get three electoral votes each: one each for their seat in the House of Representatives and two each for the seats in the Senate (the District of Columbia also receives three Electoral College votes). So, based on the U.S. Census data for 2000, which will be used to determine the Electoral College votes until 2010 when the next census is taken, Vermont gets one Electoral College vote for every 202,942 people, whereas California gets one Electoral College vote for every 615,848 people. If you look at it this way, your vote is worth more if you live in a small state like Vermont than if you live in a big state like California.

And the flip side to the winner-take-all nature of the state electoral slates is that candidates can largely skip campaigning in states they think they have comfortably wrapped up. If you're a Democratic voter in a state like Indiana that has voted Republican in 15 out of the past 16 elections, you may rightfully feel like you have no say in the outcome.

Even with all its flaws, the Electoral College system has worked remarkably well. The 2000 election was the first time in more than 100 years that the popular vote winner did not also win the Electoral College vote. So, you may as well get used to it; the only way to change the system is by Constitutional amendment—not likely to happen because it would need to be ratified by the small states, which aren't likely to give up their relative advantage.

Gush Versus Bore

George W. Bush won the 2000 presidential election by the narrowest margin in history. He became one of only four presidents ever to gain office by winning the Electoral College vote while losing the popular vote. Many maintain that he never did win the election—that it was instead handed to him by the partisan U.S. Supreme Court.

How did we get into such a mess in the first place? The campaign managers and political experts predicted a tight election from early on. Both candidates were "safe" choices: Al Gore, the heir to the Clinton legacy (for better or worse) and George W. Bush, the heir to his father's legacy (for better or worse).

> *LAUGH TRACK*
> "John Kerry will be the Democratic nominee for president. The Democrats finally found someone who is Al Gore without the flash and sizzle."
>
> —Craig Kilborn

Yet neither candidate sparked much enthusiasm from voters—that is, until after the election results failed to produce a clear-cut winner. Some described the campaign as Gush versus Bore. Bush was perceived as lacking substance and Gore was viewed as lacking charisma.

Strategists for both parties decided to solidify their base constituencies rather than try to capture swing voters and swing states. And both parties were successful in doing so, as evidenced by the stark contrast between the "red states"—a giant crescent stretching from the south through the Great Plains and the interior west—and the "blue states"—tiers of more urban states that lined both coasts—on maps of the election results.

Ultimately, Ralph Nader's third-party candidacy was the biggest difference-maker, most likely siphoning enough votes from Gore in key states like Florida to tilt the results toward Bush.

Clouds of Doubt in the Sunshine State

As the results rolled in on election night, it became clear that this one would be too close to call. Although the networks projected first Gore, and then Bush as the winner in Florida, those announcements were followed by a wave of red-faced retractions and a 3:00 a.m. Gore concession speech that was itself later retracted.

WHAT ABOUT MY LIFE?

Over the summer, John Kerry has had to deal with one of Al Gore's biggest challenges in the 2000 campaign: Getting out of the shadow of Bill Clinton.

One of Kerry's biggest challenges has been muscling his way into the media spotlight so he can let voters know who he is and what he stands for. The publication of Clinton's long-winded autobiography, *My Life*, has proven to be a major media event and, like the war in Iraq and the death of Ronald Reagan, kept Kerry's campaign out of the headlines and news talk shows.

Beyond that, the biggest impact of Clinton's book on the Kerry campaign could be rekindling the kind of anti-Clinton sentiment among conservative voters that helped George W. Bush in 2000. Kerry must be thinking, "When are we going to focus on *my life*?"

LAUGH TRACK

"Kerry is well on his way to reaching his magic number of 2,162. That's the total number of delegates he needs to win the Democratic nomination. See, for President Bush it's different—his magic number is 5. That's the number of Supreme Court judges needed to win."

—Jay Leno

Over the next 36 days, we witnessed a feverish dance of legal and political maneuvering unlike anything a Hollywood script writer could have imagined. A second "post-election" campaign was waged with more fury and, seemingly, more public participation than the "pre-election" campaign.

Because the Electoral College system calls for each state to choose its slate of electors in a manner of its own choosing, there were power struggles in Florida between local election boards, state officials, class-action attorneys, and the campaign machines behind both candidates.

It was a battle waged in the courts of Florida, in the U.S. Supreme Court, and in the court of public opinion. In the end, the lawyers took over, as they so often seem to do these days, and the case of *Bush v.*

Gore was decided by a partisan panel of Supreme Court judges. Their 5–4 decision parsed the fine distinctions of the Equal Protection Clause of the Constitution as a basis for prohibiting the Florida recounts from continuing, effectively handing the election to Bush.

Photo by Joe Raedle/Newsmakers.

Election protestors in Florida, December 2000.

WHAT IF?

The 2000 election was close in a number of states beyond Florida. A change of only 5,381 votes in four states (Florida to Gore and New Mexico, Iowa, and Wisconsin to Bush) would have resulted in an election in which neither candidate won a majority of the electoral votes, throwing it to the House of Representatives for a decision. Some voters would have welcomed that as an alternative to an election decided by the Supreme Court.

Approaching Democracy

Nearly four years later, perhaps we have enough perspective to answer the most important question raised by the 2000 election: not whether Bush or Gore actually won the election, but "Does our democracy still work?"

In the largest possible scheme of things, the answer has to be a qualified "Yes." Despite all the legal gambits and challenges, power was effectively transferred from one administration to another without a breakdown in the rule of law, without riots, killing, or use of military force.

But in other ways, Election 2000 was a wake-up call, a turbulent illustration of how easily our most cherished rights can slip away if we don't keep exercising them.

Vaclav Havel, president of the newly free Czech Republic, had this to say in his address to the United States Congress: "As long as people are people, democracy, in the full sense of the word, will always be no more than an ideal. One may approach it as one would the horizon in ways that may be better or worse, but it can never be fully attained. In this sense, you, too, are merely approaching democracy."

We are always merely approaching democracy. Our freedom depends on not standing by and letting someone else—our neighbors, our fellow citizens in Florida, or a panel of judges—cast the deciding vote.

2

"I pledge you, I pledge myself, to a new deal for the American people."

—Franklin Delano Roosevelt, delivering the first-ever nomination acceptance speech for President at a party convention, 1932 Democratic National Convention

Conventions

Enter Stage Left (or Right): Launching the Campaign at the Conventions

Once every four years, the two major political parties put on their own versions of a reality TV show: the Democratic and Republican national conventions. The national conventions are where the parties nominate their candidates for president and vice president, set an official platform, and officially launch their campaigns.

In the past, these conventions used to take on the grueling, riveting, and sometimes dirty business of choosing the parties' candidates. The conventions could be knock-down, drag-out affairs filled with intense battles for position on the podium, in the party platform, and on the convention hall floor.

Until the early 1960s, no one really knew who would emerge from the national conventions as the parties' candidates. It took 59 ballots to nominate Stephen Douglas (D) in 1860 and 46 to choose Woodrow Wilson (D) in 1912.

From Smoke-Filled Rooms to Corporate Junkets

At times, conventions could become so deadlocked between so many different candidates that party leaders had to retreat to smoke-filled back rooms and hammer out agreements that would form coalitions of delegates to back a particular candidate. In some cases, a true dark horse, such as Warren Harding (R), would emerge from these back-room caucuses as a compromise candidate.

But over the past several elections, the conventions have lost their traditional purpose of selecting the party nominees for president and vice president. Now, candidates are selected in the course of state primaries and *caucuses*—state-level party elections held in the spring to select delegates to the national nominating conventions. (*Primaries* are elections that determine who a state's delegates will be. Caucuses are state conventions where party members gather to vote for the delegates.)

The current primary/caucus/convention system isn't a very representative way to select candidates. The incumbent party typically goes with the man in office unless there's a term limit, and the "out" party candidate is usually selected by the time the Super Tuesday primaries are finished in early March.

Front-Loaded and Out of Our Control

As it currently stands, voters in a few states that happen to have early primaries wield a wildly disproportionate amount of influence on the selection process. Why should a few hundred thousand voters in Iowa and New Hampshire have such a large say in who our next president is? These states certainly aren't the most representative of our nation as a whole.

As early as 1912, Woodrow Wilson advocated changing to a national primary so that all voters have a say in who gets nominated. A series of regional primaries has also been suggested, but for various reasons—not the least of which is the amount of control the current system gives to party leaders—these reform efforts have failed.

Democratic party leaders pushed this year's primaries earlier in the year to help give them a better chance of winning the election. The goal of the "out" party—in this case, the Democrats—is to decide on an "electable" candidate as early as possible so that the focus of the campaign can change from party in-fighting to defeating the incumbent. Selecting a candidate early on also gives the party more time to raise funds for the national campaign.

John Kerry has been able to raise a record amount of money for a challenger and focus his speeches and TV ads on Bush—even as the primaries were still going on.

WHAT IF? KERRY AND THE "DEAN SCREAM"

The 2004 Democratic nomination may have been decided in Iowa on the very first day of the primary/caucus process. After finishing a distant third to John Kerry and John Edwards, Howard Dean, the early favorite, let out the now infamous "Dean Scream"—a kind of guttural roar—in a fiery speech to campaign workers after the results came in. Some analysts say it was the defining moment of the primaries, scuttling any hopes Dean may have had and launching Kerry into the role of an electable candidate—a "safe" candidate with name recognition, popular appeal, stature within the party, and strong fundraising ability.

Pre-Packaged Enthusiasm

Staging a modern national convention is like producing a week-long infomercial: It requires seasoned veterans to create a kind of canned buzz and bustle, the kind of pre-packaged enthusiasm you typically find on half-hour promos for ginsu knives, miracle stain removers, and get-rich-quick real estate schemes.

Like an infomercial, the conventions are scripted down to the minute and designed to generate a certain emotional response from the audience—in this case, confidence in the parties' candidates and enthusiasm for the party platform.

Gary Smith has produced the last four Democratic national conventions, as well as Bill Clinton's inaugural galas. It's no coincidence that his resume includes producing TV specials such as the Emmy and Tony awards and concerts for performers ranging from Barbra Streisand to Elvis Presley.

What's Love Got to Do with It?

In 2000, Al Gore demonstrated the importance of scripted image-making at the conventions when he swept his wife Tipper into a tight embrace on the podium and gave her a long, passionate kiss. This move was more about stepping out from under Bill Clinton's shadow than a spontaneous show of affection.

The infamous kiss was actually a planned stage maneuver designed to provide the news media and viewing audience with an image that carried several messages:

- ✓ I'm not Bill Clinton. I love my wife—you can trust me not to cheat on her. No impeachments here.
- ✓ I'm a spontaneous and passionate man, not the wooden policy wonk portrayed by the media commentators.
- ✓ I have the drive and enthusiasm to carry us to victory in November.

Photo by Robert Nickelsberg/Liaison/Getty Images.

Al Gore kisses Tipper at the 2000 Democratic National Convention.

Beyond the show-biz flair, the conventions have become massive fund-raising events, opportunities for the corporate mega-donors to rub elbows with celebrities and top party power-brokers. Like an elaborate puppet show, the action at the conventions takes place behind the curtain, at private parties and invitation-only galas where the real platform-building happens.

"PARTY" POLITICS

Politics is all about access and influence. If you have several hundred thousand dollars, perhaps you can make your voice heard at the Republican or Democratic national conventions this summer.

At the 2000 Republican convention in Philadelphia, you could go fly-fishing on the Delaware River with House Speaker Dennis Hastert if you donated to the Hastert's Keep Our Majority political action committee (PAC).

For $25,000, you could attend Bill Clinton's farewell dinner at the 2000 Democratic convention, complete with a limo ride to the event and an evening of conversation with a host of Hollywood stars.

A mere $1,000 earned you a spot at a power breakfast attended by Republican vice-presidential candidate Dick Cheney.

Or perhaps you were one of the lucky few who could afford a "Regents" pass at the Republican extravaganza in Philly. This exclusive ticket was reserved for donors who gave in excess of $250,000 and provided access to any party, dinner, or hospitality suite at the convention.

LAUGH TRACK

"It was reported in the paper that President Bush received a 'warm reception' from the Daytona 500 drivers. Well, sure—the drivers had never met anyone who was sponsored by more oil companies than they were."

—Jay Leno

Table 2.1 lists the top donors to the Republican and Democratic parties over the past 15 years. To find out more about who's giving how much to each candidate, go to **www.opensecrets.org**. Also, check out **www.fundrace.org/neighbors.php** to search for campaign donors by name or by Zip code.

Table 2.1

Top All-Time Donor Profiles

LEGEND: Republican [elephant] Democrat [donkey] On the fence [fence]

Between 40% and 59% to both parties = [fence]
Leans Dem/Repub (60%-69%) = [elephant]
Strongly Dem/Repub (70%-89%) = [donkey][donkey]
Solidly Dem/Repub (over 90%) = [elephant][elephant][elephant]

Rank	Organization Name	Total	Contribution Tilt 1989-2004 Cycles	Contribution Tilt 2003/2004 Only
1	American Fedn of State, County & Municipal Employees	$34,732,847	[donkey][donkey][donkey]	[donkey][donkey][donkey]
2	National Assn of Realtors	$23,913,577	[fence]	[fence]
3	National Education Assn	$23,123,574	[donkey][donkey]	[donkey][donkey]
4	Assn of Trial Lawyers of America	$22,995,216	[donkey][donkey]	[donkey][donkey]
5	Communications Workers of America	$21,833,476	[donkey][donkey][donkey]	[donkey][donkey][donkey]
6	Intl Brotherhood of Electrical Workers	$21,155,079	[donkey][donkey][donkey]	[donkey][donkey][donkey]
7	Carpenters & Joiners Union	$20,713,987	[donkey][donkey]	[donkey]
8	Laborers Union	$20,688,139	[donkey][donkey][donkey]	[donkey][donkey]
9	Teamsters Union	$20,581,715	[donkey][donkey]	[donkey][donkey]
10	Altria Group	$20,333,915	[elephant][elephant]	[fence]
11	American Medical Assn	$20,248,224	[elephant]	[elephant]
12	FedEx Corp	$20,219,244	[fence]	[elephant][elephant]
13	AT&T	$19,740,147	[fence]	[fence]
14	United Auto Workers	$19,461,085	[donkey][donkey][donkey]	[donkey][donkey][donkey]
15	American Federation of Teachers	$18,911,064	[donkey][donkey][donkey]	[donkey][donkey][donkey]
16	Service Employees International Union	$18,872,434	[donkey][donkey][donkey]	[donkey][donkey]
17	Machinists & Aerospace Workers Union	$18,287,464	[donkey][donkey][donkey]	[donkey][donkey][donkey]
18	United Food & Commercial Workers Union	$18,164,271	[donkey][donkey][donkey]	[donkey][donkey][donkey]

Rank	Organization Name	Total	Contribution Tilt 1989-2004 Cycles	Contribution Tilt 2003/2004 Only
19	Goldman Sachs	$17,712,799		
20	Citigroup Inc	$16,909,488		
21	United Parcel Service	$16,561,774		
22	National Auto Dealers Assn	$16,264,942		
23	National Assn of Home Builders	$14,832,428		
24	National Assn of Letter Carriers	$14,433,994		
25	National Rifle Assn	$14,214,992		

Note:

Rank Organization Name Total Contribution Tilt 1989-2004 Cycles Contribution Tilt 2003/2004 Only

Source: Center For Responsive Politics

Conventional Wisdom

Although the conventions have lost their traditional purpose of selecting the party nominees, they still play an important role in launching the campaign. A finely tuned convention topped off by a scintillating acceptance speech can generate the coveted post-convention bounce in the polls. The post-convention bounce is a recognized fact of presidential campaigns: a sharp, if not always permanent, increase in the newly nominated candidate's popularity in the polls.

The conventions also serve the larger purpose of unifying the party faithful in preparation for the most critical weeks of the campaign. An energized rank and file is required to dig in to the trenches for the tough work that lies ahead—getting the message out to the undecideds and getting the party base out to vote on election day.

Like Clockwork

Key events at the conventions typically unfold according to the following schedule:

✓ **Day 1—The Keynote Address.** Usually delivered by one of the party's best speakers, the keynote helps energize the delegates and sets the tone for the week ahead (unless that speaker is Bill

Clinton, who delivered a notoriously long and boring keynote speech in 1988, which almost derailed his political career).

- ✓ **Day 2—Credentials and Platforms.** Logistics such as where delegates sit and eligibility to participate are determined. The party platform is also finalized and voted on. In the past, controversial platform planks such as support for wars or civil rights initiatives have created stirring debates.
- ✓ **Day 3—The Nomination.** One of the high points of the convention. Each state delegation announces its choice (and the number of associated votes), followed by a raucous demonstration of applause and support. Neither major party has had to go beyond the first ballot to nominate since 1952.
- ✓ **Day 4—Vice President and Acceptance Speeches.** Nominating the candidate for vice president has also become a formality at the conventions. The acceptance speeches are closely-watched launching pads for the rest of the campaign. The candidates set forth their vision for the nation and outline the various party platform planks.

Photo by Erik Hromadka.

George W. Bush addresses the Republican National Convention, Philadelphia, 2000.

Timing the Bounce

Traditionally the "out" party holds its convention at the end of July and the incumbent party holds its convention in early August. The 2004 Democratic National Convention is scheduled for July 26–29 in Boston. Because of the summer Olympics, the Republican National Convention is slated for August 30–September 2 in New York, much later than the usual early August date.

LAUGH TRACK

"Today, John Kerry announced a fool-proof plan to wipe out the $500 billion deficit. John Kerry has a plan—he's going to put it on his wife's gold card."

—Craig Kilborn

This unusual timing could be a factor in the campaign. It could help John Kerry by shortening the time the Republicans have to campaign between the convention and election day. More likely, though, the timing may help George W. Bush by bringing his post-convention bounce closer to election day.

In addition, the change in dates may become a factor by bringing the Republican convention closer to September 11, keeping the contentious issues surrounding the Iraq war and the war on terrorism in the forefront during the convention and Bush's post-convention bounce.

KERRY / EDWARDS

Just after the July 4th holiday, John Kerry picked John Edwards, his former rival in the Democratic primaries, as his running mate. Edwards was hailed by Kerry supporters as a popular choice for Vice President who would help balance the Kerry ticket with his appeal as a smooth-talking, photogenic, moderate candidate from the South.

Kerry kept his choice close to the vest, announcing the VP candidate after a lengthy decision-making process that included Representative Dick Gebhardt, Iowa Governor Tom Vilsack, and, at one point, Kerry's friend, Republican Senator John McCain. The Bush campaign immediately launched a new TV ad featuring McCain after the Edwards announcement. The ad, titled "First Choice," plays up McCain's support for Bush's foreign policies in the fight against terrorism and suggests that Edwards was Kerry's second choice after McCain.

★ ***WHAT HE SAYS:***
"Boston is the place where America's freedom began, and it's where I want the journey to the Democratic nomination to be completed."

—John Kerry

★ ***WHAT HE WANTS YOU TO HEAR:***
The Democratic convention still matters—it's still a part of our electoral process.

★ ***BUT DON'T FORGET...***
Kerry strongly considered delaying acceptance of the nomination until the end of August so that he could continue campaign fundraising an extra three weeks.

Priming the Pump

The other main function the conventions still perform these days is displaying the up-and-coming stars of the party—giving the future candidates a chance to strut their stuff on the largest stage in politics.

Bill Clinton nearly derailed his own political career by delivering a long-winded nominating speech for Michael Dukakis at the 1988 national convention. His appearance on *The Tonight Show* playing a saxophone and joking about the speech was a key to repairing the damage.

In 1984, Mario Cuomo delivered his famous "Tale of Two Cities" keynote address for the Democratic national convention, which launched him on a decade of prominence in the Democratic Party. And when Gerald Ford called Ronald Reagan down to share the podium and unite the party after a divisive convention in 1976, Reagan gave a speech that so moved the party faithful, it propelled him to the nomination four years later, in 1980.

SHADOW CONVENTIONS AND SHADOWY THREATS

In 2000, a coalition of progressive political groups organized the so-called "shadow conventions," a sort of alternative to the Democratic and Republican national conventions in Los Angeles and Philadelphia.

These shadow conventions were designed to provide a non-partisan forum for discussion of issues such as campaign finance reform and the growing income gap between the super-rich and the average American.

Led by mavericks such as Senator John McCain and Arianna Huffington, the shadow conventions were promoted as an alternative to the scripted, sanitized debate at the major party conventions.

Although they may have fallen short of their goal of providing a true alternative forum, they did draw attention to the shortcomings of the current primary/caucus/convention system.

The conventions have always served as focal points for demonstrations and protests on various issues. This summer, thousands of demonstrators are planning to converge on Boston and New York, protesting on issues ranging from anti-globalization to poverty to health care. In 2000, protestors in Philadelphia erected a homeless camp called Bushville and marched with an 80-foot float called Corpzilla—a monster that devours democracy for the greater corporate good.

Both party conventions will take place in arenas situated on top of train stations, and the recent commuter train bombings in Spain have sparked heightened concerns about an attack on the conventions. But planned security measures may butt heads with the protestors this summer.

Convention planners in Boston have floated the idea of confining protestors to a "free speech zone," a small triangle of land cordoned off from the convention arena by a maze of roads, train tracks, and parking lots.

A group called "Not in Our Name" has put out a call for a million protestors to descend on New York. The NYPD and FBI are planning accordingly, including the option of calling in troops if needed, stationing snipers on rooftops, and scouring subway tunnels with bomb squads.

Analyzing a Rubber Stamp

Given the rubber-stamp nature of the conventions, what can you watch for at this year's party blowouts to help you choose between the candidates?

- ✓ Picking John Edwards as his running mate shows that Kerry was able to move beyond some original misgivings to pick a moderate Southerner who can balance his ticket and add vigor to his campaign. Edwards is the son of a Carolina mill worker and an accomplished trial lawyer. His youthful good looks have landed him in People's sexiest man alive issue.
- ✓ Edwards is 51 years old, and has served in the Senate for four years. Though Kerry himself questioned Edwards' lack of political experience during the primaries, Edwards has proven to be a skillful campaign speaker and should help Kerry in key Midwestern swing states. Edwards plays up his blue-collar roots, but he has made a fortune from medical malpractice and product liability judgments. He has a wife and three children.
- ✓ How well do Bush and Kerry handle the pressure of being in the spotlight? Although this is unlikely at today's tightly controlled conventions, are they cool under fire if something unusual happens—say, rioting at the off-site demonstrations?
- ✓ Will either candidate go out on a limb? In the past several conventions, acceptance speeches have tended to be fiery sermons filled with safe platitudes and anecdotes about the candidates' strong family values. If either Bush or Kerry has the guts to put some real policy initiatives or vision for the nation into his acceptance speech, it could be a telling sign for the campaign and how each will perform as a leader.
- ✓ Nader is running as an independent—there will be no nominating convention for him. Watch what he does during both major party conventions. Does he try to upstage either or both candidates? Does he "go negative" in any way? Or does he offer some constructive counterpoints to the party platforms? Do Bush or Kerry pick up on any of his talking points, or do they ignore him?

CHICAGO 1968—THE HEAD-BANGERS' BALL

Chicago was chosen to host the 1968 Democratic national convention for two reasons: Chicago Mayor Richard Daley's loyalty to Democratic President Lyndon Johnson and the belief that Daley could keep his city under control in the face of growing unrest over civil rights and the Vietnam War.

Daley's determination to keep the peace may have been the party's undoing. Anti-war protesters gathered to camp out in Lincoln Park because no hotel rooms were available. Instead of allowing them to stay, Daley issued an order for the park to be evacuated by 11:00 p.m.

Sure enough, at 11:00 that night, a cordon of about 1,000 police officers in riot gear marched on the park and began brutally beating anyone who remained within its bounds with nightsticks.

The violence got worse as the week progressed. There were bloody confrontations in Grant Park and along a security line set up on Michigan Avenue. The International Amphitheatre, where the unruly business of the convention was taking place, resembled an armed fortress.

The spectacle of rioting on the streets of the nation's second largest city served as a flashpoint for the growing peace movement and highlighted the disputes within the Democratic Party over support for the war.

On the final night of the convention, Hubert Humphrey tried to repair the damage in his acceptance speech, but the ongoing debates delayed the speech until after 1:00 a.m. Hardly anyone saw it, and it certainly could not erase the images of bloodshed and violence that had been beamed to the nation's TV screens from the streets outside the convention hall—images that spelled defeat for Humphrey in the November election.

As a result, the Democratic National Committee launched a movement to reform the convention nominating process. By the next election, more than a dozen states switched from party caucuses to primary elections to select their delegates. Soon primaries became the method of choice for selecting candidates. Delegates were not authorized to determine their own votes, and the conventions evolved into what we have now: a ratification of the candidates determined by the primaries and caucuses.

Above all, the parties have come to prize harmony and projecting a unified front at the conventions. Richard Nixon used this basic tenet of today's politics against the Democrats in 1968 when he stated in many of his campaign speeches that "a party divided against itself cannot govern America." Basically, Nixon was saying that the Democrats couldn't get their act together. Today, the conventions are all about showing how together the parties can be.

Photo by Santi Visalli Inc./Getty Images

Police charge outside Democratic National Convention, Chicago 1968.

"War is the continuation of politics by other means."

—Carl von Clausewitz, Prussian military strategist

The Battleground: Swing State Campaign Strategy and How It Affects Your Vote

Every vote counts, but some votes are more important than others. At least that's how the campaign strategists for George W. Bush and John Kerry look at it.

If you live in one of this year's key swing states or "battleground states," as they are often called in this year of war, you can expect to be barraged with a wave of television advertising for—and against—the candidates. You can expect regular campaign stops from W and JFK, and you can expect to have your opinion on the hot-button issues matter more than those of voters from other states.

Shaping a Battle Plan

Because the Electoral College provides for a winner-take-all system of allocating delegates from each state, candidates focus on a select number of battleground states where the margin of victory has been close in recent elections. The projected battleground states in 2004, with their associated electoral votes, are shown in Table 3.1.

Table 3.1

How a Campaign Strategist Sees Your Vote

Projected Bush States			
State	Electoral Votes	State	Electoral Votes
Texas	34	Mississippi	6
Georgia	15	Nebraska	5
North Carolina	15	Utah	5
Indiana	11	Idaho	4
Alabama	9	Alaska	3
Kentucky	8	Montana	3
South Carolina	8	North Dakota	3
Oklahoma	7	South Dakota	3
Kansas	6	Wyoming	3
		Total	**148**

Projected Kerry States			
State	Electoral Votes	State	Electoral Votes
California	55	Hawaii	4
New York	31	Rhode Island	4
Illinois	21	District of Columbia	3
New Jersey	15	Delaware	3
Massachusetts	12	Vermont	3
Maryland	10	Maine District 1	1
Connecticut	7		
		Total	**169**

Battleground States			
State	Electoral Votes	State	Electoral Votes
Florida	27	Colorado	9
Pennsylvania	21	Louisiana	9
Ohio	20	Iowa	7
Michigan	17	Oregon	7
Virginia	13	Arkansas	6
Missouri	11	West Virginia	5
Tennessee	11	New Mexico	5
Washington	11	New Hampshire	4
Arizona	10	Nevada	5
Minnesota	10	Maine at large and District 2	3
Wisconsin	10		
		Total	**221**

Note:

Electoral votes for Maine and Nebraska are not winner take all. They are allocated by Congressional district and can be split among candidates.

See Chapter 1, page **3** to learn more about how the Electoral College works.

Count yourself lucky if you live in these battleground states (or unlucky, if you hate political ads). Your vote will play a crucial role in determining who takes office in 2005. The election in each of these states is expected to be decided by a few thousand votes. In fact, early polls show the 2004 election shaping up to be just as close as the disputed election of 2000.

Targeting swing voters has become a science.

Do the Math

To win the presidential election, a candidate must win a majority of the votes in the Electoral College—that means 271 of the 538 total votes. Campaign strategists must decide how to allocate their own candidate's time and money in the most effective way. Because some states are considered firmly Democratic or firmly Republican, the strategists shift campaign resources to states that hang in the balance—the battleground states.

That means Kerry will likely spend little time in his home state of Massachusetts. Voters there have backed the Democratic candidate for President in 9 out of the past 11 elections.

Bush won't be down on the ranch much in Crawford, Texas either. The large block of Texas electoral votes is considered firmly in his control.

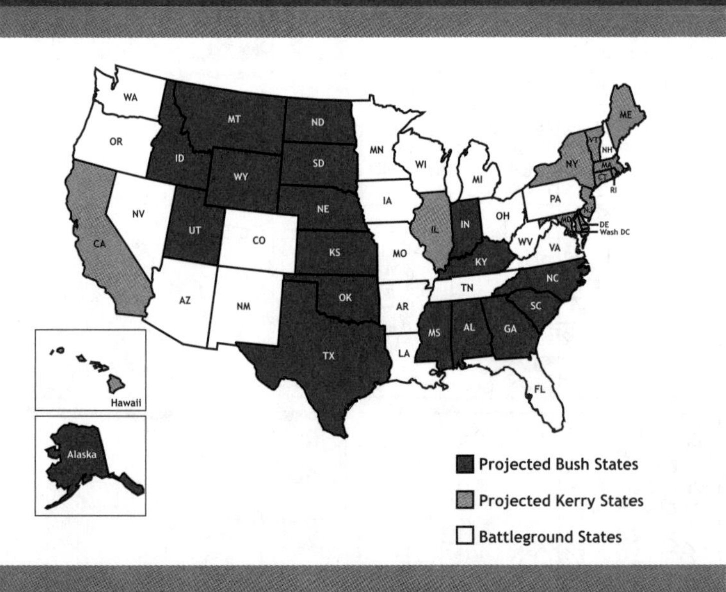

Projected Bush states, Kerry states, and battleground states. ***Analysts project Kerry to win several of the largest Electoral College states. Bush is projected to win lots of smaller Electoral College states, a pattern similar to 2000.***

Kerry Goes Big

As has been the trend for Democrats in recent elections, Kerry has a lock on several of the largest Electoral College states, including California (55 electoral votes), New York (31 electoral votes), and Illinois (21 electoral votes). That's 107 votes in only three states, more than a third of the way to 271.

Winning these large population centers means Kerry is likely to capture a high percentage of the popular vote. But can he come up with a winning formula to triumph in the electoral vote?

Bush Plays Small Ball

Bush's largest projected Electoral College state is Texas, with 34 votes. North Carolina and Georgia are next, with 15 votes each. Indiana is the only other core "Bush state" with double-digit electoral votes.

Bush's top five "gimmes" account for only 84 electoral votes, whereas Kerry's top five deliver 134. But Bush is projected to rack up a lot of other states, covering a large swath of territory from the Deep South through the Great Plains and the Mountain West. The campaign strategists predict that Bush has 18 states safely tucked away in his camp, accounting for 139 electoral votes, plus 11 of the battleground states that are projected to go his way, depending on whose survey you look at.

The Sunbelt Factor

Another factor analysts consider in projecting the electoral vote is population change. Every ten years, the distribution of electoral votes is updated to reflect the most recent census. Population growth has been most dramatic in southern and western states where Bush has the upper hand.

Table 3.2 illustrates that Bush is projected to gain five electoral votes in Texas, Georgia, and North Carolina, his top three core states, whereas Kerry is projected to suffer a net loss of two electoral votes in California, New York, and Illinois, the top three Democratic core states.

Table 3.2

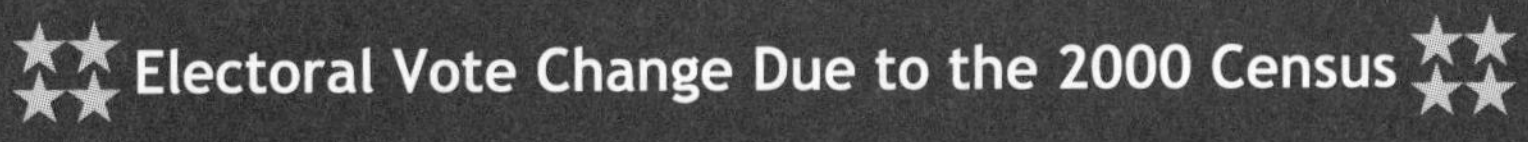

Bush States in 2000			
State	2000 Electoral Votes	2004 Electoral Votes	Change
Texas	32	34	2
Florida	25	27	2
Ohio	21	20	-1
Georgia	13	15	2
North Carolina	14	15	1
Virginia	13	13	0
Missouri	11	11	0
Tennessee	11	11	0
Indiana	12	11	-1
Arizona	8	10	2
Colorado	8	9	1
Louisiana	9	9	0
Alabama	9	9	0
Kentucky	8	8	0
South Carolina	8	8	0
Oklahoma	8	7	-1
Arkansas	6	6	0
Kansas	6	6	0
Mississippi	7	6	-1
West Virginia	5	5	0
Nevada	4	5	1
Nebraska	5	5	0
Utah	5	5	0
New Hampshire	4	4	0
Idaho	4	4	0
Alaska	3	3	0
Montana	3	3	0
North Dakota	3	3	0
South Dakota	3	3	0
Wyoming	3	3	0
Total	**271**	**278**	**7**
Net Gain in Core States			**2**

Gore States in 2000			
State	2000 Electoral Votes	2004 Electoral Votes	Change
California	54	55	1
New York	33	31	-2
Pennsylvania	23	21	-2
Illinois	22	21	-1
Michigan	18	17	-1
New Jersey	15	15	0
Massachusetts	12	12	0
Washington	11	11	0
Minnesota	10	10	0
Wisconsin	11	10	-1
Maryland	10	10	0
Oregon	7	7	0
Iowa	7	7	0
Connecticut	8	7	-1
New Mexico	5	5	0
Maine	4	4	0
Hawaii	4	4	0
Rhode Island	4	4	0
District of Columbia	3	3	0
Delaware	3	3	0
Vermont	3	3	0
Total	**267**	**260**	**-7**
Net Loss in Core States			**-3**

Content of Table credited to David Leip, www.uselectionatlas.org.

Of the key battleground states, Florida, Arizona, Colorado, and Nevada gained six electoral votes. These were all Bush states in 2000. The battleground states Gore carried—Pennsylvania, Michigan, and Wisconsin—lost electoral votes, four in all. Granted, Florida was a questionable win at best for Bush, but the bottom line in this analysis is that if things break anywhere near what they did in 2000, Kerry has a tougher road to achieving 271 based on population and electoral vote change.

YOU CAN MAKE A DIFFERENCE

Political strategists often talk about the *alignment* of states in national elections. In the most general terms, the current alignment has the Democrats controlling the most populous and most urban states along both coasts and in the upper Midwest. Republicans control most of rural America—the South, the Great Plains, and the interior west.

And some states are staunchly Republican or Democrat, no matter what the current alignment. Indiana has voted Republican for President all but one election since 1940. Massachusetts has gone the other way all but four times since 1928.

So, what should you do if you don't live in a battleground state and you're a supporter of the candidate who isn't expected to win?

Well, first of all, of course, you vote. Throwing up your hands and saying it's hopeless only makes the state you live in more firmly entrenched in the other party's camp. If the margin of victory is larger for the other guy in your state this time, you can bet that neither party will pay as much attention to your state and your opinions on the issues the next time around.

Try to build some grass-roots momentum for change in the hostile territory you happen to live in. Try to find some kindred spirits in your neighborhood, your town.

Join the party of your choice and be active in it. Vote for and work to elect local, state, and congressional candidates in your area. If no one from your party is on the ballot in a local election, run for the office yourself or try to encourage someone you would like to see in office run. You can't complain about a lack of choices if you don't do anything about it.

Even putting a bumper sticker on your car or a sign in your yard may help—at least it lets others know there are people who have other opinions about the election and what's going on in the world.

You can also try to affect the outcome of the election in battleground states. If you have friends or relatives who live in a battleground state, try to influence how they vote. Send them information about your candidate and your point of view. Get behind national efforts and organizations that represent your views on particular issues. Or, if you can, travel to a nearby battleground state and volunteer for your candidate there.

Visit the campaign Web sites for Bush, Kerry, and Nader to find out more about ways you can get involved in their campaigns, such as

- Contributing money
- Hosting or attending a "house party" or "meetup"
- Volunteering for the campaign
- Downloading campaign posters, brochures, and placards, or purchasing yard signs, pins, and other campaign gear
- View lists of unofficial grass-roots Web sites and organizations that support the candidates in battleground states—and in *your* state.

The candidates' official campaign Web sites are

www.georgewbush.com
www.johnkerry.com
www.votenader.org

Tactical Maneuvers

After deciding which states they will focus on, campaign strategists typically hit these states hard with TV advertising and grass-roots efforts such as house parties, bus tours, and the more traditional stump speeches and handshaking meet-the-voter events.

Most of the campaign budget goes to producing skillfully crafted—and often negative—TV ads, which can be shown hundreds of times in carefully selected key markets and aimed at specific issue groups such as pro-choice or seniors concerned about Social Security and Medicare.

Is Kerry a Flip-Flopper?

Bush decided to go negative early, launching a $10-million-per-week TV ad onslaught in the battleground states shortly after Kerry clinched the Democratic nomination. The ads were designed to portray Kerry as a waffling liberal who is weak on defense and wants to raise taxes.

Matthew Dowd, the Bush campaign's chief strategist, said the ads accomplished their goal. "The two things voters know about Kerry today more than anything else is that he's a flip-flopper and he's going to raise your taxes."

Oregon and New Mexico appear to be two western states where Bush has a chance to turn up the volume on his libertarian anti-government message that has worked well in other western states.

Oregon has voted Democrat the past four elections, but Gore carried state by less than 7,000 votes in 2000. Early polls showed the state to be a dead heat, with Kerry leading in urban Portland and Bush out in front in the rest of the state, where the anti-tax message has been playing well. In New Mexico, where Gore narrowly won by fewer than a 1,000 votes in 2000, the same anti-tax message might work, but it will be countered by rapid growth in the state's Latino population.

★ ***WHAT HE SAYS:***
We must "stay the course." —George W. Bush

★ ***WHAT HE WANTS YOU TO HEAR:***
Keep me in office—I'm not a "flip-flopper."

★ ***BUT DON'T FORGET…***
My course led us into the war in Iraq.

Bush can also try to steal some heartland states that went Democrat in 2000. Gore won Iowa and Wisconsin together by 9,200 votes, so either one could slip into Bush's hands in 2000 with a strong family-values message. The same strategy could apply to Michigan and Minnesota, although the large urban areas in Detroit and the Twin Cities make a shift less likely. Nader had a particularly strong showing in Minnesota in 2000, siphoning off 127,000 votes from Gore. Nader could be a big factor in tilting any of these states towards Bush this year if Nader can make himself heard on the issues without the benefit of the huge ad budgets the major party candidates have.

The "flip-flopper" ad campaign gained a lot of traction for Bush in the battleground states until it was drowned out by a nasty wave of insurgent fighting in Iraq, the noise of the 9/11 Congressional hearings, and the Abu Ghraib prison scandal—a series of events that put the Bush campaign in crisis mode and sent his approval ratings to the lowest point in his presidency.

Who's John Kerry?

Despite this opening, Kerry has had a difficult time taking advantage of the President's problems in Iraq. When the turmoil of the war dominates the news, it shoves everything else to the back burner, including Kerry's efforts to introduce himself to voters and unveil his policy initiatives.

Kerry spelled out his plan to cut the budget deficit in half on the same day Iraqi insurgents launched a series of attacks that captured parts of three cities and killed several U.S. soldiers. The policy speech was relegated to the inside of most papers and virtually ignored by the network news.

Two key prongs of Kerry's strategy depend on being able to turn attention away from the war and back to domestic and economic issues. Kerry has been trying to focus on the loss of jobs even in the midst of recovery to swing several key states his way, including Ohio, West Virginia, Michigan, and Pennsylvania.

The best demographic trend for Kerry is the rapid growth in the nation's Latino population, which could help him make inroads in Florida, Arizona, Colorado, and Nevada.

★ ***WHAT HE SAYS:***
"This administration has a truth deficit, not just a fiscal deficit." —John Kerry

★ ***WHAT HE WANTS YOU TO HEAR:***
Bush knew there were no WMDs in Iraq and sent us to war anyway. And he can't balance the budget.

★ ***BUT DON'T FORGET…***
I supported the war, but not the funds to pay for it.

Although Kerry's official fundraising total is only two-thirds of what Bush has raised, total spending on TV advertising has been relatively even if you count ads supplemented by Democratic political activist groups such as MoveOn.org and the Media Fund.

One of the ads questions why the Bush administration has spent $7 billion on Iraq: "Shouldn't America be his top priority?" Another shows a factory with Chinese characters on the smokestack and suggests that Bush's policies have led to the export of American jobs.

Shifting Sands

Much to the chagrin of the campaign strategists, the 2004 election may depend more on how each candidate responds to the shifting sands of current events than any detailed campaign strategy. Although the electoral vote analysis shows a dead heat that neither Bush nor Kerry can win by more than the slightest margin, a key event or untimely statement may turn the election into a rout for one or the other.

William Carrick, a consultant to Dick Gephardt's presidential campaign put it this way: "Anyone who says they know what's going to happen in this race is not telling the truth."

WHAT IF?

What would happen to campaign strategy if the U.S. were hit with another terrorist attack in the months or weeks leading up to the election? Many analysts say the terrorist bombings of commuter trains in Madrid three days before the election turned the outcome from the heavily favored incumbent to the Socialist Party. How would a similar attack impact election results here? Would your views of either candidate be affected?

A Volatile Mix

A volatile mix of issues—Iraq, post 9/11 terrorism, gas prices, and an economy that's shedding jobs in the midst of recovery—is frustrating efforts by both candidates to gain an edge.

Iraq is a double-edged sword for both candidates, but it could end up costing Bush the election. He is, after all, the president who pushed for the war—America's first "pre-emptive" war—in the face of strong opposition. His approval ratings sank to the lowest level of his presidency in the wake of the Abu Ghraib prison scandal. In a survey by the Pew Research Center shortly after the scandal became news, public satisfaction with national conditions fell to 33%, its lowest level in eight years.

Public response to the problems in Iraq shows that this will likely be the deciding factor in the election. Voter Carolyn Engberg from Albuquerque said, "I'd like to see a smooth transition [in Iraq], but I don't see a smooth transition coming out of this. We're so deep into this, if [the transition] fails, we'll be blamed. And if it succeeds, we'll be blamed for not doing it earlier."

BETTER OFF NOW?

While the war in Iraq may get the bulk of the media attention, jobs and the economy are still a key issue for most voters, especially in key battleground states. Bush radio and TV ads target battleground states with the message that the economy is growing again and Kerry is pessimistic, focusing on "days of malaise and the Great Depression."

Despite the economic growth, the picture isn't as bright as the Bush ads would paint it for everyone in the battleground states. Median household income is down slightly for the nation overall from 2000. Median income is up in 9 battleground states but down in 10, including the key states of Florida, Michigan, and Ohio. The election may come down to Ronald Reagan's famous challenge to voters in the 1980 campaign: Are you better off now than you were four years ago?

Michael Yost, a teacher who supports the war, said, "The bottom line is, if I don't see it, between June 30th and the election, getting better in some way, that's something that might affect my decision."

But many are still uncomfortable with the idea of Kerry as commander-in-chief. "I think he still has a lot to prove to me," said Donna Urban. "Kerry voted for the war, now he's anti-war. He's just dancing around. I'd like to see what he'd do."

Urban voted for Bush in 2000, but said he should be concerned about losing her vote this time.

ALL'S FAIR...IN WAR

War and terrorism are Bush issues. In many ways, they play into his hands: He can point to his strong defense stance, say he's the better choice for commander-in-chief, and divert attention from the social and economic policy issues Kerry wants to highlight. But the election is riding on events that may be beyond his control.

One way to look at election strategy is to find a comparable set of circumstances and candidates from the past and see whether any patterns or similarities emerge. A wartime incumbent can benefit greatly from his role as commander-in-chief—if we won the war or it's going well.

The Abu Ghraib prison scandal and the concerns about the transition of power in Iraq may make this election resemble 1980 or 1968, years in which we were embroiled in difficult, divisive situations overseas.

In 1968, President Lyndon Johnson was so drained and demoralized by the turmoil of leading the war effort in Viet Nam that he declined to run for re-election as the Democratic incumbent. Hubert Humphrey was left to try and unify a party—and a nation—that was bitterly divided over a failing and questionable war promoted by the Democratic administration. Humphrey lost the election to Richard Nixon—who ran as a peace candidate—by a narrow margin in the popular vote and a wide margin in the electoral vote.

In 1980, President Jimmy Carter was faced with the grim drama of the Iran hostage crisis. For months the nation was demoralized by pictures of Americans held captive in a faraway land and hostile mobs taking over our embassy and burning American flags.

When an attempt to free the hostages ended in a flaming helicopter wreck in the middle of the desert, Carter's fate was sealed. Carter's "crisis of confidence" speech would end up prompting a crisis of confidence *in him*. He lost to Ronald Reagan in a landslide.

/AFP/Getty Images

Scenes like this from Abu Ghraib add an unexpected crisis to the Bush campaign.

Will the shocking images of tortured Iraqi prisoners in Abu Ghraib be President Bush's version of the hostage crisis? If Bush handles the prison scandal and the transition to Iraqi power skillfully, he can point to his record as the best man to lead the country in a dangerous and uncertain era.

If Bush isn't able to bring our troops home without incident, the war will trump all other issues and render any campaign strategy meaningless.

"It has locked candidates into ridiculous positions because only ridiculous positions can be compacted into 30-second commercials."
—Senator John Danforth, (R) Missouri

4

Where's the Beef?—Deciphering Positions Behind the Media Sound Bites

The "it" Senator Danforth referred to is mass media campaigning—the art of creating 30-second or 7-second sound bites for television ads and the nightly news.

We remember the famous sound bites from past campaigns long after their policy implications or context in the campaign have been forgotten. The most effective ones stick in your head like the tune from an advertising jingle or a bad pop song: "Read My Lips, No New Taxes," "It's the Economy, Stupid," and "Where's the Beef?"

Well, the beef is not here—not in the ads or TV news clips campaign strategists use to drive voter opinions on the candidates. They are all about style over substance.

Short Attention-Span Theater

We can't put all the blame for content-free campaigning on the candidates or their handlers. To a large extent, the message is at the mercy of the medium in which it's delivered—the format drives what we see and hear, and television is the only way many voters get their news.

Television emphasizes the visual over the verbal, so the messages delivered in campaign ads and TV speeches must be kept brief and simple. Research has also shown that people focus on visual cues over auditory information when listening to speakers. As political scientist Doris Graber puts it, "People tend to believe what they see more than what they hear...You can try to counteract it by explaining what a candidate is trying to do. But people still succumb to the beautiful visuals."

We're attuned to the quick cut, short-take music video style that television (and to a large extent, radio) uses to present information and ideas. Television has always been a quick-hitting, less in-depth medium compared to print—newspapers, magazines, and especially books.

You can make yourself a more informed voter by going beyond TV to get your information on the candidates. Also, take a moment to think about the source of the article you're reading or the show you're watching. Is the source biased in any way toward a particular candidate? Does the source have a hidden agenda for the comments or positions he advocates?

DIRECT FROM THE SOURCE

Candidates offer plenty of opportunities for voters to learn where they stand on the issues. The candidates' official campaign Web sites provide the complete text of all their speeches for you to read, articles about the candidates from newspapers and magazines, as well as news releases and canned talking points for media outlets to use.

Go to:

www.georgewbush.com/News

www.johnkerry.com/pressroom

www.votenader.org/media_press

The campaign Web sites include complete statements from the candidates on where they stand on the issues.

You can also search the complete text of all candidate speeches by going to **www.vote-smart.org**. Type the name of the candidate you want to search for in the Find Your Representative text box at the left side of the page and then click Go. (You can find Ralph Nader by entering "Nader" in the box.)

After the candidate's Vote-Smart page appears, click on the Speeches and Public Statements link to search for comments by keyword.

The Vote-Smart Web site also contains complete voting record info for each candidate, organized by year and by issue, as well as a complete list of ratings given to each candidate by special interest groups.

Late-Night Laughs

A Pew Research Center poll found that almost as many young Americans aged 18–29 get their political news from *The Daily Show* and *Saturday Night Live* as from regular network news programs (21% to 23%). Shows such as Bill Maher's late, great *Politically Incorrect*, started blurring the lines. Now comedians such as Dennis Miller, Al Franken, and Janeane Garofalo are getting in on the act with their own political talk shows on cable. Beyond the punch lines, viewers value the ability of these entertainers to cut through the canned messages with their humor.

Candidates have picked up on this trend: John Edwards launched his Democratic primary campaign on *The Daily Show*, Howard Dean tried to control the damage from his "Dean scream" speech by doing a "Top Ten List" on *The Late Show with David Letterman*, and John Kerry has tried to loosen up his stuffy, aristocratic image by riding a Harley onto the set of *The Tonight Show*.

Ever since Bill Clinton salvaged his career by wailing on the sax with Arsenio Hall's band, candidates have realized the importance of being viewed as relevant and hip. The downside to all the fun: You won't hear the candidates delving into much detail on how to pay for Medicare and Social Security or how to cut the budget deficit on these shows.

Photo by Kevin Winter/Getty Images

Kerry revs up his campaign on Leno.

MATCH GAME 2004

Test your knowledge of the 2004 presidential candidates (or at least the images they are trying to project) by matching the following sound bites with the candidates who said them.

Answers can be found at the end of this chapter, on page 66.

Score: 1–5—Read on, you need help. 6–12—Nice job, you've got media savvy. 13–15—Political junky, get a life.

1. "I don't think the culture has changed to the extent that the American people or the Congress would totally ban abortions."

2. "I believe and have fought for the principle that we should protect the fundamental rights of gay and lesbian couples—from inheritance to health benefits. I believe the right answer is civil unions. I oppose gay marriage and disagree with the Massachusetts court's decision."

3. "We need to get out of there (Iraq) as fast as possible because we are the magnet for increasing guerilla warfare and increasing entry by Al Quaeda and others, just the opposite of what we were told was going to happen."

4. "I was in favor of disarming Saddam Hussein, and I'm glad we did. There's no ambivalence."

5. "If we restrain spending, even though we're at war, even though our economy is still clunking along, if we react responsibly, we can return to a balanced budget, something I want, as early as 2004. But tough choices on Capitol Hill have to be made."

6. "It's going to take a while to implement the Medicare bill. It's a complex piece of legislation. After all, it's the first modernization since Lyndon Johnson signed Medicare in the mid-60s."

7. "The whole tax system is a mess. Corporations have to be taxed fairly. They shouldn't be allowed to get into tax shelters or go to Bermuda or fool around with all their loopholes. That's one. The second is we should shift taxes away from work and on wealth."

8. "This isn't going to be some kind of 'We're like them, they're like us, wishy-washy, mealy-mouth, you can't tell the difference' deal."

9. "I actually did vote for the $87 billion before I voted against it."

10. "If a charity is helping the needy, it should not matter if there is a rabbi on the board, or a cross or a crescent on the wall, or a religious commitment in the charter. The days of discriminating against religious groups just because they are religious are coming to an end."

11. "It isn't pollution that's harming the environment. It's the impurities in our air and water that are doing it."

12. "The death penalty does not deter, is discriminatorily applied, probably has led to the execution of innocent people, and should be abolished."

13. "Major combat operations in Iraq have ended. In the battle of Iraq, the United States and our allies have prevailed."

14. "We need to now go to the moon here on Earth by setting America on the course to energy independence."

15. "And clearly it is not just our best interests, it is in the best interests of the world to make it clear to Saddam Hussein that he's not going to get away with a breach of the '91 agreement that he's got to live up to, which is allowing us to know that he has dismantled his weapons."

Earned Airtime

The old-style network news programs also do their part in shaping the format and content of the campaign. Because of time constraints, they have to be selective in what they feature each day. Candidates have to muscle their way onto Dan Rather's TelePrompTer past a smorgasbord of international, health, crime, science, and Hollywood features—all crammed into less than thirty minutes.

This scramble for "earned" airtime is perhaps the single most important advantage George W. Bush enjoys. As president, anything Bush does is news. Any policy statement Bush cares to make on any issue is covered by the full White House press corps. Bush has made good use of this advantage, using his role as commander-in-chief of U.S. forces in Iraq to stay in the nation's news spotlight, even as Kerry attempts to introduce himself to voters and define his candidacy.

Kerry's advantage—and the advantage of every challenger—is that he can highlight faults or problems the nation currently faces and attribute those to the president, while talking about the things that he will do to correct the matter if voters give him a chance.

Candidates and campaign managers realize that this earned airtime will be edited down to brief sound bites, and try to construct their speeches accordingly, breaking off the key points they want to make into brief, catchy phrases.

Copyright: www.cartoonstock.com.

Caught in the Crossfire

Beyond the network news shows, a host of "squawk box"–type shows on cable news networks such as the *O'Reilly Factor, Beltway Boys, Scarborough Country,* and *Crossfire* create a constant drone of instant sound bite campaigning. Talk radio shows such as Rush Limbaugh promote the same type of discussion. The Bush and Kerry campaigns must stay on top of the 24/7 sparring with a cadre of reporters, specialists, experts, and ex-military and government staffers who weigh in on debate after heated debate.

Although Fox coverage is typically aligned with Bush as the conservative, Republican candidate and CNN and NPR are typically aligned with Kerry as the liberal, Democratic candidate, Bush clearly enjoys the benefits of incumbency on all the networks because everything he does is news.

LAUGH TRACK

"The election is in full swing. Republicans have taken out round-the-clock ads promoting George Bush. Don't we already have that? It's called Fox News."

—Craig Kilborn

Sound Bite Savvy

The following section contains a sampling of sound bites from the three major candidates on five hot-button issues to help you cut through the rhetoric and get a handle on their positions. For a comprehensive summary of the candidates' positions on these and other key issues, turn to the chapters featuring each candidate (Chapters 8–10), as well as Chapter 11, "Candidate Comparison Guide," on page 157.

Abortion

Bush

What He Says: "I will lead our nation toward a culture that values life."

What He Wants You To Hear: I'm opposed to abortion, with exceptions for incest, rape, and life-threatening risk.

The Bottom Line: Will work toward legislation such as the Partial-Birth Abortion Ban Act, which he signed. Will not choose Supreme Court justices based on abortion rights issue.

Kerry

What He Says: "Never have women been assaulted in their citizenship here at home or womanhood around the globe as they are by this administration."

What He Wants You To Hear: I'm pro-choice, with no exceptions.

The Bottom Line: Voted NO on the Partial-Birth Abortion Ban Act—says it erodes *Roe v. Wade* and a woman's right to choose. Will choose only Supreme Court justices who support the *Roe v. Wade* decision.

Nader

What He Says: "I don't think government has the proper role in forcing a woman to have a child or forcing a woman not to have a child."

What He Wants You To Hear: I'm pro-choice—this shouldn't be an issue at all.

The Bottom Line: Hasn't had to stick his neck out by voting for or signing a bill, but his statements are consistently pro-choice.

Economy

Bush

What He Says: "The tax relief we passed is working. See, I believe that when people have more money in their pocket, they will then spend, or save, or invest, and that causes the whole economy to grow, which then helps people find a job."

What He Wants You To Hear: I'll cut your taxes and create more jobs.

The Bottom Line: Will work toward further tax cuts for individuals and businesses, as well as curbing government regulation of business. The Jobs and Growth Act he signed may have sped up recovery from the recession, but job growth has been weak and the budget deficit is growing.

Kerry

What He Says: "It's a recovery for the people in the corporate boardroom. It's a recovery for corporations, to some degree, by compacting, by increasing productivity. But if you go across America, it's not a recovery."

What He Wants You To Hear: Are you better off than you were four years ago? The answer is no. We're losing jobs because of Bush.

The Bottom Line: Voted NO on balanced-budget Constitutional amendment (1997), but voted NO on bill that would prioritize tax cuts over debt-reduction. This is a hot-button issue for Kerry because he can run on what he *will do* after he gets in office, whereas Bush has to defend the current economy and job situation. Kerry vows to add three million jobs in his first 500 days in office and roll back tax cuts for the wealthiest Americans while retaining what he calls middle-class tax cuts: the child tax credit and the reduced marriage penalty.

Nader

What He Says: "The complexity and distortions of the federal tax code produce distributions of tax incidence and payroll tax burdens that are skewed in favor of the wealthy and the corporations, further garnished by tax shelters, insufficient enforcement, and other avoidances."

What He Wants You To Hear: Nader-speak for saying the corporations and the wealthy get too many tax breaks.

The Bottom Line: Would change the law to tax wealth instead of wages. Would increase the minimum wage. Would increase investment in infrastructure, require equitable trade, and work toward a renewable energy policy. Emphasis on reducing tax advantages of large corporations.

Iraq/Terrorism

Bush

What He Says: "Hundreds of thousands of service men and women are deployed across the world in the war on terror. By bringing hope to the oppressed and delivering justice to the violent, they are making America more secure."

What He Wants You To Hear: Iraq is but one battle in the war on terrorism—linking Iraq to 9/11 attacks. We were justified in invading Iraq even though no WMDs were found there, and it's a tough situation for our troops.

The Bottom Line: Although we achieved the overthrow and capture of Saddam Hussein, we're still embroiled in a war that may be difficult to get out of. It remains to be seen whether we have deterred terrorists by invading Iraq or merely stirred up a hornet's nest that will provoke even more attacks.

Kerry

What He Says: "Whether Saddam Hussein is gone or not, we went to war in a rush, we went to war without a plan for winning the peace. This has been a disorganized, haphazard effort."

What He Wants You to Hear: I'm a better commander-in-chief than Bush is. I understand how to wage a war, and I would not have invaded Iraq without complete U.N. backing.

The Bottom Line: Voted YES on initial Iraq invasion, but later voted NO on funding the war. Would seek to involve the U.N. in the transfer of power in Iraq and would withdraw quickly, while training an Iraqi security force. Would use diplomatic measures to crack down on Al Quaeda operations in Iran.

Nader

What He Says: "The war in Iraq was developed from a messianic militaristic determination turned by a closed mind, facilitated by a cowering Congress and opposition Democrat party and undeterred by a probing press. Bush is acting in effect as a selected dictator, not listening to any of the many retired admirals, generals, and foreign-policy experts who have warned against the war."

What He Wants You To Hear: I've been against this war from the beginning.

The Bottom Line: Opposed the invasion and occupation of Iraq from the start and linked it to a drive for Iraqi oil. Played up connections in the Bush administration to big oil companies, including Condoleeza Rice as a former director of Chevron. Says Bush misleading U.S. on the basis for war is an impeachable offense. Criticized attack on Afghanistan in the wake of 9/11.

Education

Bush

What He Says: "I refuse to give up on any child. And the No Child Left Behind Act is opening the door of opportunity to all of America's children."

What He Wants You To Hear: I'm a compassionate conservative—I believe the children are our future.

The Bottom Line: Although the intent of holding schools accountable is certainly one that most people agree on, the emphasis on assessment and testing has led to a narrowing of focus at schools to passing the state exams. Schools struggle to meet No Child Left Behind mandates without federal funds. Bush favors vouchers as an alternative for students who attend failing schools.

Kerry

What He Says: "I want standards and accountability. But you cannot do it without the resources, and you also can't do it in a way where you turn the schools into testing factories."

What He Wants You To Hear: I supported No Child Left Behind, but Bush tax cuts undermined funding for it. Also, I support the teachers' unions.

The Bottom Line: Wants to increase federal funding to support No Child Left Behind. Also wants to increase funding to reduce class size, build new school facilities, and support teachers with better pay. Would give college tax credits and start a national service program to help students work to pay for college.

Nader

What He Says: "Students should learn, as the core curriculum, developing civic skills, learning how to practice democracy...and the arithmetic, reading, and writing will be a by-product."

What He Wants You To Hear: Don't focus on standardized testing; focus on producing good citizens.

The Bottom Line: Opposed to standardized testing and favors a focus on teachers and students. Does not favor punishing schools or students that don't meet testing standards. Supports alternative public school choices such as magnet schools, schools-within-schools, as well as home schooling. Wants to get rid of Channel One and reduce commercialism in schools.

Gay Marriage

Bush

What He Says: "If judges insist on forcing their arbitrary will upon the people, the only alternative left to the people would be the Constitutional process. Our nation must defend the sanctity of marriage."

What He Wants You To Hear: I'm opposed to gay marriage.

The Bottom Line: Bush favors a Constitutional amendment defining marriage as solely as the union between a man and a woman, while letting states define their alternative legal arrangements for gays. Bush has tried to strike a "morally traditional, socially inclusive" formula, not actively rolling back protections for gays such as spousal benefits while in office, but opposing changes in areas such as marriage. Appointed an openly gay man to head the Office of National AIDS Policy, but refused to accept support of a gay Republican group.

Kerry

What He Says: "I believe the best way to protect gays and lesbians is through civil unions. I believe the issue of gay marriage should be left to the states."

What He Wants You To Hear: I'm opposed to gay marriage, but I'm unwilling to actively legislate against it.

The Bottom Line: Opposes gay marriage but said he would vote against a Constitutional amendment outlawing it. Disagrees with Massachusetts Supreme Court opinion allowing gay marriage in his home state. Favors civil unions as the method of guaranteeing gay couples' legal rights and says these are state, not national issues.

Nader

What He Says: "This should not become a major issue in the campaign because none of the candidates should be boorish enough to oppose love and commitment under stable relationships."

What He Wants You To Hear: I'm the only one who supports gay marriage.

The Bottom Line: Touts his record as a supporter of rights for all minority groups, including women and gays. Says gays should have the right to marry as well as the right to civil union.

LAUGH TRACK

This election is shaping up great. Our choices are a guy who always has second thoughts or a guy who's never had a first thought.

—Jay Leno

The Art of the Sound Bite

In spite of its faults, the sound bite can serve as a powerful, defining force for a campaign. The best sound bites are simple and direct. They roll off the tongue and capture the essence of the issue or person they're describing.

Several presidential elections have turned on effective use of the sound bite.

George Bush Sr. used a couple of good ones to soundly defeat Mike Dukakis: "A kinder, gentler nation" served to separate him from Ronald Reagan's policies, and "Read my lips, no new taxes" powered him into office, although the lip readers decided not to re-elect him when he reneged on the promise and raised taxes after he was elected.

"Tippecanoe and Tyler too," launched William Henry Harrison into office as a war hero, whereas Woodrow Wilson won in 1916 based on the slogan, "He kept us out of war." Ironically, Wilson didn't. One year later we entered World War I on the side of the Allies.

Some sound bites have become famous in a losing cause. "Where's the beef?" helped Walter Mondale fend off Gary Hart in the 1984 primaries, but he couldn't translate the slogan into the general election, where he lost to Ronald Reagan.

READ MY LIPS: WE NEED A SLOGAN

When it comes to political slogans, neither Bush, Kerry, nor Nader have lit up the campaign trail with anything memorable. The outcome of many past elections has turned on effective use of slogans such as "Morning in America," "Read my lips, no new taxes," or "It's the economy, stupid." This year, the absence of a compelling slogan is apparent from the fact that both Kerry and Bush are still searching for something new.

Bush changed the slogan on his campaign web site from "Steady Leadership in Times of Change" to "Yes, America Can!", a rather noncommittal phrase that doesn't say anything about Bush himself.

Kerry has cycled through so many clunky slogans (including "Let America Be America Again," "Change Starts Here," "The Real Deal," "Bring It On," and "A Lifetime of Service and Strength") that some supporters have suggested he define his campaign in the simplest way possible, with the catchy phrase "I'm Not Bush."

A couple of Kerry sound bites have floated to the surface. "Truth Deficit" seems to get some play as a rhetorical link between questions about Bush's handling of the Iraq war and the growing budget deficit. Kerry is also fond of reminding people that he's "a fighter," tying in his policy's on jobs and the economy to his experience as a Vietnam war veteran, though it hasn't congealed into a full-blown slogan yet.

The candidates seem to be better at developing jabs for each other. Nader calls Kerry a Crypto-Republican. Kerry has gained some traction is using the phrase "Misery Index" to refer to economic troubles, and Bush has had great success with the tag "flip-flopper" to describe Kerry. Kerry has responded to the Bush campaign slogan "Steady Leadership in Times of Change," by calling it "Stubborn leadership, not steady leadership."

The most clever phrase any of them has come up with so far is Bush's twist on Kerry's slogan "The Real Deal." Bush's campaign web site prominently features a section called "John Kerry: the Raw Deal."

MATCH GAME 2004 ANSWERS

Here are the answers to the quiz:

1. George W. Bush
2. John Kerry
3. Ralph Nader
4. John Kerry
5. George W. Bush
6. George W. Bush
7. Ralph Nader
8. John Kerry
9. John Kerry
10. George W. Bush
11. George W. Bush
12. Ralph Nader
13. George W. Bush
14. John Kerry
15. John Kerry

"The best people, the best thinkers, generally adapt with a change in circumstance."
—Mary Beth Cahill, Kerry campaign manager

And the Survey Says... How Your Opinion Can Shape Positions on the Issues

Are opinion polls a means of ensuring that politicians stay connected to the views and needs of their constituents, or are they a tool that campaign managers use to tailor media messages and even manipulate election results in their favor?

Yes, polls help candidates—and voters—stay informed about what the nation's voters want and think. But polls are also an integral part of the media feedback loop—the finely tuned marketing machine that's designed to sell candidates to us in much the same way we are sold a tube of toothpaste, a six-pack of beer, or a new car.

Start with a Benchmark

Campaign managers have several different kinds of voter feedback tools at their disposal. Most campaigns start with a benchmark poll—an extensive survey designed to spec out the candidate's platform on all the most pertinent issues. Consultants and candidates use the data from the benchmark poll to plan campaign strategy and then compare it with later follow-up polls as a gauge for how well the campaign is going.

If a follow-up survey indicates that the campaign strategy isn't working as well as planned, the candidate's message and platform are adjusted accordingly. Campaign managers can mine a steady stream of poll data to formulate a platform and message that appeal to the broadest spectrum of voters and can spin on a dime to fit the latest public opinions.

Panel surveys help the campaign manager follow shifts in public opinion throughout the course of the campaign, and nightly tracking polls monitor public opinion on current events as well as the impact of new ads from the candidate and his opponent.

LAUGH TRACK

"According to the recent polls, Bush has a slight lead over John Kerry. So today, Bush hung a banner over the White House saying, 'Mission Accomplished.'"

—David Letterman

Tracking poll results give the campaign manager and the candidate their cues for creating "crafted talk," the media messages they will use in the next day's campaign speech, press release, or interview with the pundits.

The objective is to shape the media message by being responsive—in a sense, feeding the views and opinions of the public back to the voters, telling them what they want to hear. The broadcast media is the candidate's accomplice in delivering the message—preferably in the form of free news coverage or in the form of paid political ads.

MARGIN OF ERROR

Public opinion polls typically provide a "margin of error" figure along with their results—something like "the margin of error for this poll is plus or minus four percentage points." What they are trying to tell us is that their methods of polling are sound and the result is an estimate: It could be off either way by about four points.

So, a poll showing Bush leading Kerry by two percentage points is really a dead heat because the lead is within the statistical margin for error. But the main word to see in the phrase "margin of error" is the word "error." As scientific as the pollsters make the information sound, polls have a number of variables that can skew the results and make them just plain *wrong*.

In the 2000 election, all the major TV networks and the Associated Press projected Al Gore the winner of the Florida vote at 8:00 p.m. Eastern time, based on early exit polls that skewed toward traditionally Democratic precincts. By 2:00 a.m., they had switched gears and projected Florida for Bush. By the next morning, the race was declared too close to call.

Some allege the networks were biased toward Gore and began calling Gore states earlier than Bush states, thus dampening Republican voter turnout. The networks also called Florida before all the panhandle precincts were closed, curbing turnout in a traditionally Republican part of the state.

Whether the projections actually affected the outcome in 2000, the networks are likely to be more careful about making early projections based on poll results. And you should also remember to take the polls with a large grain of salt this fall as you follow the election and decide who will get your vote.

Focus on the Intangibles

Consultants rely on focus groups to dig into the motivations behind the hard data that opinion polls provide. They gather a specially selected group of voters in a room and ask them about everything from the color of a candidate's clothes to the cadence of his speech—and maybe a few questions about their opinions on the issues as well.

In some cases, focus group participants are hooked up to electronic monitors that measure their emotional responses to words, phrases, and intagibles such as a candidate's "likability" or "believability."

Another way of gathering instant feedback on an issue or position is to use "dial meter" focus groups. Participants hold "perception analyzers," electronic dials that can be moved left or right—indicating negative or positive—in response to what they see or hear on a screen. The results are tallied and graphed instantly, providing a rich source of emotional gut reaction to the candidate's appearance or message.

Shape the Outcome

Perhaps the most effective—and underhanded—way to influence the outcome of an election is the use of what is called "push polling." Under the guise of a national market research firm, voters may be contacted by phone and asked to answer a survey about the election. The polling organization then asks questions that are designed to influence the voter's opinion about an opposing candidate.

A typical push poll question might sound something like this:

"Would you be more or less likely to vote for candidate X if you knew that the murder rate in his state went up nearly 15% during his term as governor, while more than 3,000 convicted felons were released because of prison overcrowding?"

Push poll questions are designed to target precise segments of voters who can swing elections. Push polls are typically used in the final days or weeks of the campaign, sometimes as a means of suppressing voter turnout for an opposing candidate.

Most candidates don't use push polling, but it's something to be aware of and watch out for during the final phase of the campaign.

Leadership Versus Followership

How much Bush and Kerry use opinion polling data to shape their positions on the issues could become an issue in and of itself during this campaign.

Using a barrage of TV ads in key battleground states, Bush has been successful in shaping public opinion about Kerry as "flip-flopper," someone who changes his views based on the latest polls. Conservative political action committee Web sites such as FlipFlopper.com help drive the message home. FlipFlopper.com lists Kerry's changes in position on issues such as the war in Iraq, the marriage tax penalty, and the Patriot Act.

★ *WHAT HE SAYS:*
"The family has it. I don't have it." —John Kerry, commenting on the Chevy Suburban SUV in which he has been seen riding.

★ *WHAT HE WANTS YOU TO HEAR:*
That's my wife's truck. I'm an environmentalist.

★ *BUT DON'T FORGET...*
Bill Clinton's famous line: "That depends on what your definition of 'is' is..."

A Leader for Uncertain Times

The flip-side of the Bush strategy is the slogan touted on the official Bush campaign Web site: "Steady Leadership in Times of Change." The message the Bush campaign has crafted is Bush is a leader; Kerry is a follower. We need a leader during an uncertain time when we are at war and faced with terrorist threats on our homeland.

The message has been largely successful in driving public perception, portraying Kerry as an opportunistic career politician with no principles, who follows the shifting tides of opinion polls.

Despite setbacks and casualties in Iraq, Kerry has not been able to gain ground in the polls. Because of Bush's position as the wartime incumbent and commander-in-chief, Iraq and terrorism remain Bush issues—even if the news is bad in these areas, they may help Bush by keeping Kerry's domestic agenda out of the news.

LAUGH TRACK

"A new poll shows that most college students would rather have President Bush as a roommate than John Kerry. Yeah, but which one would you rather cheat off of in class?"

—Jay Leno

Steady or Stubborn?

Kerry has countered with a twist on the Bush slogan, asking the question: "Steady Leadership, or Stubborn Leadership?" The Kerry message has been prompted and supported by the ongoing investigation of the nation's preparedness for the 9/11 attacks as well as damaging portraits of the internal workings of the Bush administration in books such as Richard Clarke's *Against All Enemies* and Bob Woodward's *Plan of Attack.*

Kerry's goal is to portray Bush as a man who was hell-bent on invading Iraq—even before the 9/11 attacks and to the detriment of tracking down Osama Bin Laden, whereas Kerry is a more intelligent leader who can adjust his strategy according to the nuances of international diplomacy and the developments in current events.

The objective is to create fear and concern over Bush as a sort of rogue president, who will do whatever he darn well pleases—a man who led us into an unnecessary and ill-planned war in Iraq in spite of strong opposition at home and abroad.

Bush Can Morph Too

The Bush campaign knows the value of the opinion polls in waging a winning campaign. When the furor over the Woodward and Clarke books coincided with setbacks in Iraq and the Abu Ghraib prison abuse scandal, Kerry used the opportunity to lay out a plan for transfer of power in Iraq that would rely heavily on the involvment of United Nations oversight and peacekeeping troops.

Shortly thereafter, Bush announced that his own transfer of power plan would include a larger role for the U.N., something largely absent from his earlier plans. This shift has all the markings of a reaction to tracking polls that showed a positive response to U.N. involvement.

In effect, Bush negated the Kerry advantage on this issue by co-opting Kerry's position. This is an example of how the opinion polls tend to drive candidates closer together on issues, sometimes resulting in positions that are virtually indistinguishable. The end result is elections that are won or lost on matters of style, not substance: "likability" and "believability."

WINNING THE WAR ON TERROR...IN THE POLLS

With polls showing Bush's approval ratings at new lows and tracking down in all areas but the war on terror, the Kerry campaign went on the offensive in New Mexico, a key battleground state.

Kerry used the polling info to launch an ad that touts his 1997 book *The New War: The Web of Crime that Threatens America's Security,* and describes him as "author of a strategy to win the war on terror."

The Bush campaign responded quickly to protect it's lead on this key issue. An ad called "Yakuza" was aired on TV in New Mexico, shooting down the Kerry book as focusing on a Japanese crime syndicate. The ad's voiceover states, "John Kerry says he's 'author of a strategy to win the war on terror?' . . . against the Yakuza. Never mind al-Quaeda. Says nothing about Osama Bin Laden. Calls Yasser Arafat a 'statesman.'"

No doubt the Kerry and Bush campaigns will watch the poll results closely to see if the battle of the ads has had any effect.

Making Your Opinion Count

Imagine you get the call: Your phone rings around dinner time one evening, maybe interrupting your meal or favorite TV show, and the voice on the other end of the line says they'd like to ask you some questions about your preferences on the candidates and certain issues. What will you do?

Against the Odds

Don't hang up. This isn't a sales call—it's an opportunity to make your opinion known. Even national opinion polls use very small, representative samples of "likely" voters, often as few as 750 to 1,000 participants each.

Taking part in a poll—whether it's independent or conducted by a campaign consultant—has an impact on the decisions candidates make about their positions on the issues. In some ways, participating in a poll can have a greater impact on the election result than casting your vote. Consider the statistics: Your opinion in a poll is one out of 750–1,000. Your vote in the election is one out of about 100,000,000.

Most opinion surveys take less than half an hour of your time—about the same time it takes to vote. Opinion polling organizations use random phone-number dialing to get a random sample of voters—the odds are against participating in a survey. Just be aware of push polling—questions that are phrased in such a way so as to influence your opinions about a certain candidate. You can answer these surveys—typically with brief "yes" or "no" answers—but remember that the purpose of the surveys is more to influence your vote than to gather information. Don't hesitate to hang up if you think you're being push polled.

CAN YOU HEAR ME NOW?

The people who conduct opinion polls have a big problem on their hands: cell phones. Because the computerized random dialing programs include only land lines, cell phone numbers aren't reached by the polls. As more people switch to cell phones as their primary phones, polls have a more difficult time reaching a representative sample of voters.

Noted pollmaker John Zogby said, "When I started in this business in 1984 they [response rates] were averaging about 65%. Now we're down around 33 or 35%."

Aside from the fact that fewer people pick up the phone or want to respond when polling organizations call, leaving cell phone users out of the sampling group skews the poll results. In 1948, pollsters used telephone surveys to wrongly project that Dewey would beat Truman by a wide margin, but not everyone had phones at that time, and those who did tended to be more well-off and vote Republican. How much does the "cell phone variance" skew today's poll results? Relying on land-line–only polling may skew survey results to older and more rural residents—those who are less likely to use a cell phone as their primary phone.

Pollsters say their methods still produce valid results, but many predict they will have to use other methods within the next 10 years. The rise of Internet polling is one way to go. They may also turn to more paid participation as response rates continue to fall.

Take Charge

If you don't want to wait for a polling organization's computer to random-dial your phone, you can go online and participate in a Web-based poll. Or you can take charge and contact a candidate directly to voice your opinion.

To send the Kerry campaign an e-mail message, go to **www.johnkerry.com/contact/**. Click the General Comments link in the Email Addresses box at the right side of the page. You can then fill out a form with your name, e-mail address, and the message you want to send. You can also select from a drop-down list of subjects.

You don't need to include your address or phone number if you prefer to keep that information private. Also, note the Receive Kerry Campaign Emails check box. Click this box to uncheck it if you don't want to receive e-mails from the Kerry campaign.

To send the Bush campaign an e-mail, write to **BushCheney04@GeorgeWBush.com**. Or go to **www.georgewbush.com/ContactUs/** and fill out the e-mail form, including your message. Note that if you fill out the Bush form, there is no way to opt out of receiving e-mails from the campaign.

To contact the Nader campaign by e-mail, go to **www.votenader.org** and click the Contact link at the bottom of the home page. This takes you to an e-mail form you can use to send the Nader campaign your thoughts or comments. Note that you will be added to the Nader e-mail list and will receive e-mail updates from the Nader campaign.

There's no guarantee that the e-mails sent to these sites will be read—least of all by the candidates themselves. But there is a chance that your message will be searched for key words, be read by a campaign worker, and in some way contribute to shaping the platform of the candidates—certainly more of a chance than if you do nothing.

"What negative advertising does is get your supporters committed and excited. Those who are indifferent are so turned off that they are less likely to vote, as are people who are for the other candidate—not only does it help you, but it depresses turnout."

—Dean Michael Mexay, DePaul University

6

Wallowing in the Mud: Obscuring the Issues by Going Negative

Why do candidates use negative campaign tactics? Because they work.

Negative ads are effective because they drive up the negative perceptions of voters about an opponent and they take the opponent "off message," forcing him to respond to the attack. In the jargon of the political consultants, negative campaigning creates "FUD": fear, uncertainty, and doubt about an opponent.

The important thing for you as a voter to understand is how to evaluate the various types of negative campaign tactics and recognize how they affect voter perceptions on different levels. Then you can make informed decisions about the issues behind the ads and where the candidates stand on them.

Bring Out the Hammer and Tongs

One of the goals of negative ads is to depress voter turnout for the candidate's opponent. The other primary goal is to energize the candidate's core group of voters. Negative ads have also proven effective at pulling undecided voters into a candidate's camp because swing voters may be more likely to respond to emotional appeals: If they're undecided on the issues, they may vote based on character or the "lesser of two evils."

All these factors serve to depress voter turnout in general, however, because voters tire of the barrage of negative statements designed to tear down both candidates.

LAUGH TRACK

"John Kerry described his Republican critics as 'the most crooked, lying group I've ever seen.' Now, that's saying something, because Kerry's both a lawyer and a politician."

—Jay Leno

Jeff Parker—caglecartoons.com

Attack Early and Often

This year's campaign has "gone negative" much earlier than normal for a variety of reasons:

- ✓ Negative campaigning often happens in very tight races—and this year's election is shaping up as a repeat of 2000, a statistical dead heat.
- ✓ The Democrats front-loaded their primaries so they could find a presumptive nominee much earlier in the year. This enabled them to focus on fund-raising for Kerry and avoid a lengthy fight among themselves. Kerry's campaign was able to target Bush—rather than Edwards or Dean—with ads as early as March.
- ✓ Bush has a war chest estimated at more than $215 million. Incumbents typically benefit most from negative campaigning because they are able to sow doubt about a new challenger—the fear of the unknown. This was Bush's strategy in the initial barrage of negative Kerry ads: Defining Kerry before he had a chance to do so himself. Kerry has plenty of money too, and he has learned the lesson of Mike Dukakis: Never fail to respond to an attack.
- ✓ The belligerent tone is a carry over from the disputed 2000 election. The never-ending campaign is now a fact of life—there is no longer any downtime after the election is over for the president to simply become our leader, our chief executive. Political pundits such as Rush Limbaugh, Bill O'Reilly, Al Franken, and Michael Moore have a vested interest in keeping the debate going and keeping the tone nasty.
- ✓ Bush is a polarizing figure. To a great extent the Kerry campaign—really, the campaign of whomever the Democrats ended up nominating—is more anti-Bush than pro-Kerry, an "Anyone But Bush" attitude. The campaign message is "We need to get behind Kerry because we need get Bush out of office." This kind of approach lends itself to negative campaigning.

- ✓ Political action committees and special interest groups create their own ads that are nearly always anti-opponent, not pro-candidate. Soft money groups such as MoveOn.org and the Media Fund create ads that are specifically tied to voting Bush out of office. Often, these ads are more vitriolic than anything the candidates themselves would ever produce or approve.

Negative Ads or Deceptive Ads?

We tend to think of negative campaigning as a one-size-fits-all brand of mud-slinging. But some types of ads that are typically characterized as "negative" can be useful in framing a candidate's position on the issues: "He's for abortion and I'm not." Just because an ad targets an opponent, that doesn't mean it's negative.

LAUGH TRACK

"President Bush is not fazed by other candidates' war records. He said, 'I may not have fought in Vietnam, but I created one.'"

—Craig Kilborn

With that said, ads that mention opponents in any way are more likely to distort an opponent's position or take an opponent's statement out of context to make a point. Instead of putting ads that target an opponent under one "negative" blanket, it's helpful to think about these ads as fitting into one of the following categories:

- ✓ **Contrasting**—An ad that targets the opponent on an issue or set of issues, such as the abortion example. These ads are the most constructive of the "negative" ads. They delineate what a candidate stands for—just be careful to look for distortions and false claims.
- ✓ **Attack**—An ad that targets the opponent on a personal issue or character trait: "He's a liar." "He cheats on his wife." "He flip-flops on the issues." These are more serious than the contrasting ad, because they shift the campaign away from issues and focus on personal matters. However, character issues are important factors in choosing our leaders, and many voters respond to these ads if they feel the claims are not false.

- ✓ **Deceptive**—Both contrasting and attack ads can be deceptive. If they make false claims, twist an opponent's words, or take them out of context, deceptive ads can come back to haunt the candidate that uses them.
- ✓ **High-Road**—Ads about ads. These ads attack the attacker, basically saying "shame on you" for launching a negative campaign and defending the candidate who makes these ads from the claim(s) of the first ad. Running these ads isn't as bad as launching a negative campaign, but they still perpetuate the back-and-forth volleying. They also take the focus away from the issues.

KERRY GETS MOORE THAN HIS MONEY'S WORTH

John Kerry has raised the most campaign funds of any presidential challenger in history, but his ad budget has also been supplemented by free anti-Bush publicity from several high-profile books and movies.

First there were the two best-selling books by Richard Clarke (*Against All Enemies)* and Bob Woodward (*Plan of Attack*) delving into the Bush administration's handling of the 9/11 attacks. Both books were published around the time of the congressional 9/11 hearings and criticized Bush's response to the security threat.

Next came the PR circus surrounding Michael Moore's film "Fahrenheit 9/11." The film's first buzz was generated when Disney declined to distribute it. Then the movie won the Palme d'Or at the Cannes Film Festival, priming the pump for a top showing at the box office. Kerry couldn't spend any amount of money to buy the negative PR for Bush that the books and movie have generated.

Ready, Aim, Attack!

Here's a sampling of negative ads from Bush, Kerry, and the PACs. See if you can fit each ad into one of the four categories already described. Also, look for statements you think might be deceptive by being twisted or taken out of context, and then check the section called "Spin Cycle" immediately following for an analysis of each ad.

You can also view these ads online by going to **www.quepublishing.com/everyvotecounts/**.

Bush Ads

The following Bush ads are designed to define Kerry for the voters as a "flip-flopper" who doesn't stick to his word, who will raise taxes, and is weak on defense. Are they successful? You be the judge.

"Weapons"

Voiceover: "As our troops defend America in the War on Terror, they must have what it takes to win."

Voiceover: "Yet, John Kerry has repeatedly opposed weapons vital to winning the War on Terror: Bradley Fighting Vehicles... Patriot Missiles... B-2 Stealth Bombers... F-18 Fighter Jets, and more."

Voiceover: "Kerry even voted against body armor for our troops on the front line of the War on Terror."

Voiceover: "John Kerry's record on national security: Troubling."

Spin Cycle

This is a contrasting ad on the issue of defense spending. It highlights Kerry's record of voting against defense spending bills, which is valid—especially the October 2003 vote against supplemental funding after voting for the Iraq war resolution. The distortion comes in the portrayal of Kerry's votes as being against the troops themselves—denying them body armor or vehicles they need to protect themselves. Many of the votes happened as far back as 1984, and all but one were not tied to the Iraq war.

In addition, funding for many of the weapons listed in the ads was part of complex budget legislation, so Kerry's voting no on the bill did not necessarily mean he was opposed to funding those specific weapons.

"Tell the Truth"

John Kerry: "So I'm going to try and change the discussion and just tell the truth to the American people. I never ran one negative advertisement against my opponents in the primaries. And I haven't run negative advertisements yet."

Graphic: September 3, 2003: John Kerry releases his first advertisement...an attack against the president.

Graphic: 57% of John Kerry's ads have directly attacked the president...

[John Kerry's ads pop up on screen.]

Graphic: More than 73% of all of John Kerry's ad budget has been dedicated to negative attacks...John Kerry has spent over $17 million on negative ads...

Graphic: John Kerry's 21 negative advertisements have run more than 28,285 times...More than 28,285 times...

John Kerry: "Tell the truth to the American people...Tell the truth to the American people...Tell the truth to the American people...And I haven't run negative advertisements yet. My advertisements in this race are positive."

Spin Cycle

A double-whammy: an attack ad (calling Kerry a liar) that also takes the high road. The message is, "Shame on you, John Kerry, for attacking the president, and then lying about it." But isn't this an attack ad too?

"Doublespeak"

Voiceover: "John Kerry says: 'A lot of people don't really know who I am.'"

Voiceover: "Well, actually, a lot of people do."

Voiceover: "Kerry's hometown paper says, 'In his continuing effort to be all things to all voters...John Kerry is engaging in a level of doublespeak that makes most voters wince.'"

Voiceover: "*The Wall Street Journal* said Kerry's tax plan 'would mean increasing the tax burden again, which would likely kill the recovery.'"

Voiceover: "On Iraq, *The Washington Post* said 'Kerry's attempts to weave a thread connecting and justifying [his] positions are unconvincing.'"

Voiceover: "The *Union Leader* says Kerry has 'waffled' on historic education reforms he supported in 2001, but now opposes."

Voiceover: "And the non-partisan *National Journal* magazine ranks Kerry the most liberal member of the Senate—more liberal than Hillary Clinton or Ted Kennedy."

Voiceover: "John Kerry's problem is not that people don't know him. It's that people do."

Spin Cycle

A combination attack ad and contrasting ad. Portrays Kerry as a waffler, who doesn't stick to his guns, while also trying to define Kerry as a "liberal" who will raise taxes. This is probably the most effective of the ads: positioning Kerry as a "liberal," which motivates the Bush base, and defining him as a "flip-flopper," which sows doubt among undecided voters.

But the changes in position can be for valid reasons: Kerry initially supported Bush's No Child Left Behind plan, and then withdrew support after it became clear the plan lacked adequate funding.

Kerry Ads

The following Kerry ads are designed to present Bush as someone who over-promises and under-delivers, a reckless and irresponsible leader. Are they convincing? You be the judge.

"Little George's First Budget"

Teacher: "George, it looks like you're having a little trouble with your math..."

Little George: "What do you mean?"

Teacher: "Well, your budget numbers don't add up."

Little George: "Well, they're close enough."

Teacher: "George, you've overspent by $6 trillion."

Little George: "Oh, is that a lot?"

Teacher: (sighing) "Well, yes, it is...Okay, here, you forgot to pay for the cost of making your tax cut permanent...that adds $2.2 trillion alone."

Little George: "Well, I really want it."

Teacher: "And now here, you spent another $616 billion for your prescription drug plan."

Little George: "I know, but the drug companies need the money."

Teacher: "And see this plan to privatize Social Security?

Little George: "Yeah?"

Teacher: "Well, that costs $1.4 trillion."

Little George: "I know, and I don't even like the program."

Teacher: "Well, George, if you're going to spend all this money, you have to figure out a way to pay for it."

Little George: "Well, you just watch. When I'm president, I'm gonna spend as much money as I want."

Voiceover: "And that's exactly what George Bush did..."

A combination attack ad and contrasting ad. By dreaming up a fictional classroom scene between a "Little George" and his teacher, the ad highlights the growing budget deficit under Bush while portraying Bush as petulant and dim-witted—a leader who lacks sufficient understanding to balance our national budget. This also plays up the Kerry theme of Bush providing "stubborn leadership, not steady leadership." The deception here is obvious: Even if the numbers are valid, the scene itself is a complete fabrication.

"No, Mr. President"

Voiceover: "George Bush's latest ad says he's being attacked for attacking the terrorists. No, Mr. President. America is united against terror."

Voiceover: "The problem is, you declared 'mission accomplished,' but had no plan to win the peace and handed out billions in contracts to contributors like Haliburton."

John Kerry: "I'm John Kerry, and I approved this message because we can't go it alone in Iraq. We have to share the burden with other countries. We shouldn't be cutting education and closing firehouses in America while we're opening them in Iraq."

Like Bush's "Tell the Truth" ad, this is a combination high road and attack ad, but it goes a bit further to also spell out Kerry's position on the issue. It's kind of like an "I'm sorry, but..." statement in an argument. The message here is, "I'm sorry I attacked you in my last ad, but it wasn't really an attack because you deserved it. And, by the way, I'm right and my position is 'We can't go it alone in Iraq.'"

Political Action Committee Ads

The following ad from the Media Fund, a political action committee run by former Clinton strategist Harold Ickes. This organization is not officially associated with the Kerry campaign, but all its ads are anti-Bush.

Credit: Gary Markstein and Copley news Service

Factory

Voiceover: [showing a factory smokestack] "During the past three years, it's true George W. Bush has created more jobs."

Voiceover: [as camera pans back to show Chinese words on factory] "Unfortunately, they were created in places like China."

Voiceover: "Bush's policies have encouraged the loss of more than three million jobs. He supported tax breaks to corporations that shipped jobs overseas."

Voiceover: "George W. Bush is taking our country in the wrong direction. It's time to make America work—for every American."

The "Factory" ad is of course really a Kerry ad, although it's paid for by a PAC. This is a clever twist on the jobs issue. The deception here is two-fold: Linking corporate tax breaks to sending jobs overseas and ignoring the flip-side—the many benefits of a global economy. The reality is that many companies get tax breaks but they aren't tax breaks *to encourage* sending jobs overseas. The ad's wording makes it sound that way.

Let Me Count the Ways

Of course, there are many ways to slam your opponent besides TV ads. Be aware of phone calls from campaigns that deliver a message in the guise of a survey—so-called "push polling."

Most political speeches have some sort of negative reference to the opponent, and the news talk shows are filled with poisoned back and forth sound bites.

To learn more about how candidates use sound bites and push polls, see Chapter 4, "Where's the Beef—Deciphering Positions Behind the Media Sound Bites," **p.XXX**, as well as Chapter 5, "And the Survey Says…—How Your Opinion Can Shape Positions on the Issues," **p.xxx**.

Third-party Web blogs and the candidates' official Web sites have proven to be useful negative campaign tools. The Bush site in particular has some clever gadgets that slam Kerry, including a "Kerry Gas Tax Calculator" and a "John Kerry Travel Tracker," that claims to show "why John Kerry is wrong for your state."

In all of these cases, keep in mind the lessons from analyzing the TV ads in this chapter: Watch for exaggeration, simplification, and statements taken out of context. Understand that the truth is always more complex than what you can read or see in 30 seconds.

7

"Character is like a tree and reputation like its shadow. The shadow is what we think of it; the tree is the real thing."

—Abraham Lincoln

A Question of Character: Leadership, Integrity, and Personality as Deciding Factors

As you consider the candidates' positions on the issues, keep in mind that there is more to electing a good president than choosing between competing laundry lists of platform positions. There can be no doubt that the candidates' positions on the issues are of vital importance to making an informed decision about who to vote for—the second half of this book is devoted to mapping out those positions in detail.

But we are electing a person—a human being—to serve in what is undoubtedly the most demanding job on Earth.

As Abraham Lincoln said in the quote that opens this chapter, all the ads and speeches about Kerry's waffling and Bush's "truth deficit" are the shadow—the reputation. How Bush and Kerry handle themselves in the months leading up to the election are the tree—the true character—especially for Bush, whose handling of the war in Iraq will be the defining moment of his administration.

What's underneath, the makeup of each man and how he would address a crisis such as Abu Ghraib are the true definitions of character, and certainly a deciding factor in this year's election.

Character Matters

Most voters have an instinctive sense that sound character is one of the most important—if not *the* most important—qualifications for a strong president. But there are many reasons why an election can swing from one candidate to another—changes in the economic and foreign policy situation of our country, different approaches to the hot-button issues of the day. Even so, for many undecided or independent voters, a large part of the decision-making process comes down to a gut reaction on "likeability" and "believability," as the pollsters like to put it. And, of course, there is that other intangible: good, old-fashioned charisma.

That charisma—the ability to project a strong flair for leadership—made both Ronald Reagan and Bill Clinton popular choices for president, despite their differences on policy issues and in other character traits. The public response to Reagan's recent death highlights the fact that even his political opponents admired him and considered him to be a man of strong character. Clinton, who spent his final days in office concerned about what his "legacy" would be, can only wonder whether he will be remembered the same way.

As a voter, you should also consider that even though most policy positions are developed with wider input from party leadership and larger organizations, the way those positions are implemented often depends on the individual character and agenda of the president.

In this election, you are choosing someone who will have to steer us through a series of unforeseeable crises and challenges. Determining how a leader will stand up to the pressure and demands of these situations is just as important as judging his stated position on the issues in the run-up to an election.

Farrington—caglecartoons.com

Peggy Noonan, speechwriter and biographer for President Reagan, makes a strong case for a candidate's character being the most important factor in determining who will be the better president:

"In a president, character is everything. A president doesn't have to be brilliant; Harry Truman wasn't brilliant, and he helped save Western Europe from Stalin. He doesn't have to be clever; you can hire clever. White Houses are always full of quick-witted people with ready advice on how to flip a senator or implement a strategy. You can hire pragmatic, and you can bring in policy wonks."

"But you can't buy courage and decency, you can't rent a strong moral sense. A president must bring those things with him. If he does, they will give meaning and animation to the great practical requirement of the presidency: He must know why he's there and what he wants to do. He has to have thought it through. He needs to have, in that much maligned word...a vision of the future he wishes to create."

"But a vision is worth little if the president doesn't have character—the courage and the heart—to see it through..."

LAUGH TRACK

"President Bush is on a bus tour right now, visiting small towns in Michigan and Ohio, because he says, and I quote, 'I find it really fun to go to a place where people don't expect the president to come.' So the next place he's going—a bookstore."

—Jay Leno

The Vision Thing

The Bush campaign has made "the vision thing," as George Bush, Sr., liked to put it, the keynote of its ad blitz against Kerry: Steady Leadership versus the Flip-Flopper, sowing FUD (fear, uncertainty, and doubt) in voters' minds about a relatively unknown challenger. It's all about creating an impression, a storyline, to wrap around each candidate.

The Bush campaign is built around framing the issues for a country that's portrayed in crisis and under attack, and then asking who you would rather have lead us: The man who carried us through 9/11 and responded with force, or the man who waffled on support for the Iraq war?

But touting the steady leadership that directed us into an increasingly messy and unpopular war could prove fatal to Bush's chances in November. The spiraling scandal over the Abu Ghraib prison debacle and the ongoing difficulty of extricating our troops from Iraq threaten to turn the war into a public opinion disaster—both at home and around the world.

The war that Bush pushed so hard to carry out could prove to be the lasting legacy of his administration—and the millstone that drags him down.

LAUGH TRACK

"Insiders have begun voicing serious concerns about how Kerry's conducting his campaign. One aide told the *New York Times* that while Bush's message of 'steady leadership' has remained consistent, Kerry has gone through six different messages in the 18 months he's been running, including, at one particularly desperate juncture, 'Kerry: Health care jobs for the troops' environment.'"

—Jon Stewart

A "Big-Issue" Election

The dilemmas we face in Iraq are exactly the type of leadership challenge and defining moment that test a president's character. The 2004 election is a big-issue election—the 2000 election was a small-issue election. No matter how much Kerry and the Democrats want to switch the debate to social and economic issues at home, the way Bush handles the events in Iraq may well determine the outcome at the polls in November.

The decisions Bush makes on the evolving events in Iraq are not so much policy decisions as tests of his character—his moral and ethical judgment and his ability to lead the nation through a foreign-relations crisis of his own making. He was, after all, the man who pushed so hard for starting the war, against the wishes of many voters at home and many allies abroad.

★ *WHAT HE SAYS:*
"The actions of these few people do not reflect the hearts of the American people...It's also important for the people of Iraq to know that in a democracy, everything is not perfect, that mistakes are made." —George Bush, addressing Arab TV networks about the Abu Ghraib prison scandal.

★ *WHAT HE WANTS YOU TO HEAR:*
I'm sorry. I apologize.

★ *BUT DON'T FORGET:*
White House spokesman Scott McClellan later said: "The president is sorry for what occurred and the pain it has caused."

When asked why Bush had not apologized, McClellan replied, "I'm saying it now for him." Bush eventually apologized for the abuse several days later.

Can Kerry turn the bad news from Iraq to his favor? Possibly, but he has to tread carefully. He doesn't want you to view him as undermining the president or our armed forces. And even though Kerry has an active, and perhaps even heroic, service record in Vietnam to compare with Bush's stay-at-home National Guard service, Kerry's post-duty protests and testimony before the Senate about committing atrocities while in Vietnam leave him little leverage in the prison war-crimes scandal.

Keefe—caglecartoons.com

SPIN TO WIN—DAMAGE CONTROL AND COUNTERATTACK MARKETING

Presidential campaigns have evolved into a series of attacks and counterattacks involving the candidates' reactions to current events and issues of the day.

A candidate's success on election day is linked to his ability to run damage control on situations such as Kerry's ribbon-tossing episode and war record (which occurred 30 years ago but became "news") and Bush's handling of the Abu Ghraib prison-abuse scandal.

Democrats have been unsatisfied by the Kerry campaign's lack of a killer instinct on Iraq—his inability to "go for the jugular"—as well as his tendency to create sound bites the Bush campaign can use against him, such as the statement, "I actually did vote for the $87 billion before I voted against it."

President Bush faces a minefield of damage control situations from the Iraq war. The Abu Ghraib prison scandal threatens to turn into a Watergate-type affair, dragging on for weeks and months through the relentless pressure of 24/7 media coverage, congressional hearings, and independent investigations—all of which provide the Democrats with ample opportunities to spin and attack.

How Do They Stack Up?

One way for you to think about the character of both Kerry and Bush is to compare the two men to presidents of the past. How do they stack up to our past leaders, and who are they most like in personality and psychological makeup?

Bush Equals Truman, Bush, Sr.,...or Johnson

The Bush campaign's "Steady Leadership" slogan brings to mind image-making in the mold of Harry Truman: A tough SOB who stands up for what he believes and follows through with it—no matter what others think. As Truman said, "Here I am, here's what I stand for—here's what I'm going to do if you keep me in the job. You decide."

The Kerry campaign has turned the Steady Leadership slogan around, calling it "Stubborn Leadership," evoking Truman's legendary stubbornness. There certainly are some similarities between Bush and Truman in the biggest picture: down-to-earth, anti-intellectual leaders with a dogged pursuit of their own particular vision and having no particular qualms about using military force.

Truman did not hesitate in nor lose sleep over his decision to drop the atom bomb on Japan. He readily identified the Communists as our post-war enemy and challenged them on several fronts, launching us into the Korean War. Bush was relentless in pushing for the war in Iraq, selling his view of the necessity for war and never backing away from his plans in the face of strong opposition—of course, Bush supporters view this as a plus; his detractors see it as a blind vendetta.

Bush's solemn evocation of patriotism and duty in the wake of 9/11 helped carry the nation through one of its worst crises. Yet, there are many differences between Truman and Bush. Truman's courage was honed on the battlefield and through tough years as a Missouri farmer. Bush comes from a wealthy and privileged family—some would say privileged enough to avoid having to fight in Vietnam.

WHAT IF?

Richard Nixon's spin on the Watergate break-ins went from "we didn't do it" to "the CIA set us up" to "all presidents have done this" to "John Dean did it" to "I am not a crook." What if Nixon had simply admitted the mistake right up front and promised to address the problem rather than trying to spin and deny it?

Would Watergate have simply blown over and now be remembered as nothing more than another election-year campaign dust-up? Or were Nixon's abuses of power so numerous they would have caught up to him in the end?

Shadowing Dad

The fact that George W. has followed so closely in his father's footsteps can't be overlooked. Both attended Andover prep school, and then Yale, returned to Texas as oil men, entered politics, and eventually made it all the way to the presidency.

But whereas George Bush, Sr. seemed to possess the comfortable grace of a patrician leader, George W. has had a bumpier road: A less-than-heroic war record when compared to his father, failed oil business and alcohol problems in his early life, and a controversial—some would say illegitimate—presidency.

George W. has shadowed, and tried to live up to, his father all the way through. Their careers follow similar paths, including the invasion of Iraq.

LAUGH TRACK

"President Bush apologized on TV to Iraqi prisoners. I don't know if the apology was sincere, because at the end, he says, 'I'm George Bush and I approve of this naked pyramid.'"

—Craig Kilborn

A Uniter or a Divider?

Perhaps Bush is more like Lyndon Johnson, a folksy Texan and wartime president who was a polarizing figure—either much loved or greatly hated. Johnson has been described by biographer Robert Dallek as "not just liked and disliked but adored by some and despised by others. Some people remember him as kind, generous, compassionate, considerate, decent...Others describe him as cruel, dictatorial, grandiose, even vicious."

Like Bush, Johnson was saddled with an unpopular and divisive war—the war in Vietnam. Although it was not of his own making, Johnson believed in it and viewed those who opposed him and the war as disloyal and unpatriotic.

Johnson was determined to follow through with the war effort in the face of growing opposition, in part because he was driven by inner demons to prove his worth, but in the end the war destroyed his administration.

Bush has shared the same determination in Iraq: He believed in the reasons behind the war and viewed it as the right thing to do for the country. But will the war he created end up costing him the election?

Kerry as FDR...or Gore Part II

Kerry has been painted by Bush supporters as an "instant waffle," a political opportunist who changes his position on any topic or issue when it's convenient for his own personal benefit. But perhaps Kerry can be viewed as an updated version of Franklin Delano Roosevelt: a compassionate intellectual who sees that there can be any number of possible solutions to a problem.

FDR defied categorization by those who wanted him to stick to a particular plan or ideology. There was no coherent policy; he tried whatever he thought would work. To get the country out of the Great Depression, he spent money and he saved money; he tried direct relief programs, and he tried work programs.

He was always looking for a new idea—a different way to do things. And perhaps this openness to ideas, this eclectic approach, was the right way to face the multitude of challenges presented by a severe depression and a global war.

Kerry too seems open to any idea that might work—or even sound as if it works. Whatever fits the bill. This has been viewed as a weakness—a lack of conviction or integrity. But perhaps the lack of dogma, the openness to hear what other people think, is a trait that could help a leader adapt in difficult and complex times.

Kerry's intellectualized ramblings and his tendency to split hairs or exaggerate when he's in a tight spot with the politically correct, ("The family has it. I don't have it," he said, referring to the Chevy Suburban he has been seen riding in), puts him in the same wonky realm as two failed Democratic candidates: Al Gore and Michael Dukakis.

One way to look at Kerry is as Gore lite—a bit friendlier and less filling, but still the same kind of know-it-all who will keep talking at you until he either changes your mind or bores you into submission.

Nader as the Outsider

One of the reasons voters have a hard time picturing Ralph Nader as president is because he has never held office as an elected official—and there is probably a very good reason for that. Nader is most effective as an outsider—a change agent who isn't tied in to the established power structure.

By definition, Nader loses some of his appeal when voters think of him actually holding the office of president. Compromise doesn't seem to be part of his demeanor: How would he work with Congress to get things done? He also seems to be a lone wolf: Who would he select for his cabinet and how well would he function as a leader?

For these reasons and more (including all the electoral barriers an independent candidate faces in our two-party system) it's difficult to view Nader as anything more than a shrewd advocate for change who's using the election as a platform to advance his agenda.

"We'd Ride Horses, Play Tennis"

Undecided voters, who have mixed views on Bush and Kerry's stands on the issues, may well go with their gut feelings this election: Who do they like more? Who do they trust more as a leader?

One poll-taking group, the University of Pennsylvania's Annenberg Public Policy Center, conducted a focus group designed to find out how voters view Bush and Kerry as persons. They asked focus group members to envision what spending a weekend with Bush and Kerry would be like.

Jeanne Oberti, an office assistant who leans Republican, seemed enthusiastic about spending a weekend at the Bush ranch in Crawford, TX: "I think they would be interested in my opinions...We'd ride horses, play tennis."

Another focus group member, a retired teacher and a Democrat, also had a positive view of hanging with W: "I didn't vote for him, and I don't think I will...and yet I think I would have a great time down there at his house."

LAUGH TRACK

"Please explain to me why John Kerry sounds more [irritating] telling the truth than Bush sounds when he's lying. How is that possible?

—Jon Stewart

Other comments show why Bush has a favorable public image with many voters: "First of all, they (the Bushes) would be good listeners, smile a lot. Then, George and I would talk about sports...We'd play some golf and then talk very little politics, mainly sports."

The time with Kerry was harder for the focus group members to pin down. They speculated that it would be "a lot of fun" and "a little more intellectual." Some added comments about skiing and snowboarding or a "big place in the country."

REMEMBERING THE GIPPER

The death of Ronald Reagan in June stopped the presidential campaign in its tracks and shifted the nation's focus for a full week to the life of the man many are calling the greatest president of the twentieth century.

While many critics still don't agree with Reagan's economic or defense policies, it's hard for anyone to deny the enormous impact Reagan had on the political landscape as well as the direction of our nation in the wake of the setbacks we suffered during the 70s. Most will agree that Reagan's character and vision set him apart from other politicians. Even if you didn't agree with Reagan's policies, it was hard not to like him as a person and to appreciate his steadfast pursuit of the goals he believed in.

Reagan's death was one of many events in the past several months to shift attention away from Kerry's bid to oust Bush, and the national celebration of Reagan's accomplishments during the mourning period was certainly a big boost to the Bush campaign. Bush is a direct political descendent of Reagan through his father, who served as Reagan's Vice President. Recounting Reagan's success in bringing down the Soviet Union has helped focus attention on Bush's aggressive foreign policy during a time when many are questioning the value of the Iraq war.

But beyond policy, the remembrance of Ronald Reagan helps emphasize the importance of character in a president. Reagan's optimism and sense of hope infected the country when it was needed to counter an era of malaise and discontent. Even Reagan's staunchest adversaries remembered him as a man who could disagree with them yet still remain cordial, polite, and full of humor. Voters may well be looking for this type of character and courage when they vote in November.

The "We Need a Change" Vote

Many of the Annenberg focus group members mentioned the Iraq war as the key issue of the campaign. One said, "It wasn't [Kerry's] policy to get us in there, so maybe he'd come in there with a fresh approach. I'm getting very anti-Bush...I just see us in a mess that I don't see us getting out of. I don't know why we get into these foreign countries and think that they will welcome us."

Bush supporter Vincent Vassalluzzo said he hopes Bush will make the right decisions in Iraq, "even if it means losing the election."

Clearly, this man is looking for a show of character. If voters don't see that on display and the war goes badly, the "we need a change" vote may swing the election to Kerry.

Part II

Comparing the Candidates

8

"It was classic George Bush: 'I made up my mind and here's what I'm gonna do.'"
—Terry Johnson, college friend of George W. Bush, about the day Bush quit smoking, cold turkey.

George W. Bush: The Incumbent

George W. Bush quit smoking the same way he quit drinking—the same way he does most things: cold turkey, all or nothing, black or white.

In his famous speech after the 9/11 terrorist attacks, Bush framed his approach to tracking down the terrorists and our relations with other countries in straightforward, concrete terms: "Either you are with us or against us." No middle ground.

A Defining Moment

The September 11 terrorist attacks are widely viewed as the defining moment of Bush's presidency. He showed steely determination and great strength of leadership during the tense and fearful weeks following the attacks, and his approval ratings soared to all-time highs.

Bush entered the White House as an isolationist on foreign policy, in favor of withdrawing U.S. troops from abroad, but the terrorist attacks changed that stance dramatically. Guided by the interventionist views of Vice President Dick Cheney and Defense Secretary Donald Rumsfeld, Bush responded to the attacks quickly and decisively.

He launched an invasion of Afghanistan, ousting the Taliban regime which supported and hosted Al-Quaeda leaders and training camps within weeks. However, the effort to track down Al-Quaeda leader Osama bin Laden has been unsuccessful to date. He established the Department of Homeland Security in an effort to coordinate intelligence and public safety efforts in the U.S.

There was broad public support for these initiatives in the wake of the attacks, but controversy has surrounded the Patriot Act legislation, which gives government expanded powers of surveillance and arrest.

Bush has accomplished a great deal during his term in office, in large part due to the support of a Republican-controlled Congress. Despite the critics, the bi-partisan No Child Left Behind act was a significant piece of education reform legislation, and his tax cuts may well have softened the blow of the post-dot-com recession. The military actions in Afghanistan and Iraq ousted two of the world's most repressive regimes.

Bush is a personable and charismatic leader, with strong "people" skills that have made Americans confident in his leadership in fighting terrorism post-9/11. But Democratic critics of the increasing budget deficit and a growing outrage over the war and the Abu Ghraib prison scandal may shake voter enthusiasm for a second term in a year where gas prices have skyrocketed, the economy is still unsteady, and Iraq remains a volatile and hostile place for U.S. troops.

★ ***WHAT HE SAYS:***
"In our grief and anger we have found our mission and our moment." — George W. Bush, after September 11 attacks.

★ ***WHAT HE WANTS YOU TO HEAR:***
We are unified as a nation in the fight against terrorism.

★ ***BUT DON'T FORGET:***
Bush has used the anti-terror campaign to launch several controversial policies such as the invasion of Iraq and the Patriot Act.

Photo Credit: Getty Images

George W. Bush speaks to rescue workers, fire fighters, and police officers in the rubble of the World Trade Center, September 14, 2001.

GEORGE WALKER BUSH—FACT FILE

43rd President of the United States

Born: July 6, 1946, New Haven, Connecticut

Nickname: “Dubya,” “43”

Education: Yale (B.S., 1968), Harvard (M.B.A., 1975)

Religion: Methodist

Marriage: Laura Welch, on November 5, 1977

Children: Barbara Bush (1981), Jenna Bush (1981)

Career: Businessman, public official

Political Party: Republican

Writings: *A Charge to Keep* (1999)

Pets: Two dogs, Spot and Barney, and a cat, India

Hobbies: Reading, jogging, fishing, and watching baseball games

LAUGH TRACK

"One critic in the *L.A. Times* said John Kerry looks like he is thinking too much. Well, this is one place President Bush has him beat."

—Jay Leno

Son of George Bush

George W. has followed in his father's footsteps all his life, and the challenge of living up to his father's legacy has proved to be both a blessing and a curse. The fact that he was George H. W. Bush's son has opened doors for him throughout his life, but it also proved to be a shadow he sought to escape in his early career.

George W. Bush is the eldest of former President Bush's five children, and he was certainly the most freewheeling, although he felt pressure to fit into the mold of his father's definition of success. "All I ask," George W. once said to a reporter when running for governor of Texas, "is that for once you guys stop seeing me as the son of George Bush."

Photo Credit: Getty Images

George W. Bush with his father in Midland, TX, 1954.

Governor Dubya

In 1994, he ran against incumbent Texas Governor Ann Richards, the woman who mocked Bush's father at the 1988 Democratic Convention with her famous line, "Poor George, he can't help it—he was born with a silver foot in his mouth." It's unclear whether a desire to avenge the attack on his father or a desire to prove himself on a political stage were motives for George to run, but he relied on his wife Laura to help him sort through his decision to enter the race.

"She wanted to make sure this was something I really wanted to do and that I wasn't being drug in as a result of friends or 'Well, you're supposed to do it in order to prove yourself, vis-á-vis your father,'" Bush said.

Bush proved to be a popular candidate and a successful politician. He won the election handily, defeating Richards by staying on message and building a coalition of traditional conservatives as well as women and Hispanic voters. His platform included welfare reform, tort reform, and giving local school districts more control over funding. He also vowed to improve the state's juvenile justice system through building more facilities and applying tougher sentences.

As governor in Texas, a state larger than most countries, Bush laid the groundwork for his first run for the presidency. His two and a half terms in office were marked by controversy over the number of death-row executions prompted by his get-tough stance on crime.

Bush pushed accountability in schools through mandated statewide achievement testing. He also promoted "faith-based" government social services initiatives as a foundation for his "compassionate conservatism." Bush was the first Texas governor to be re-elected to consecutive four-year terms, and he won his re-election in 1998 with 69% of the vote on the strength of his reputation during his first term for bipartisan leadership. He had become a political force in his own right, and he prepared to take the next step in following his father's path by running for President in 2000.

What You See Is What You Get

Bush's political agenda is informed by his Texas and family roots: His faith-based initiatives are inspired by his born-again Christian spirituality. His emphasis on defense is a result of his family's service in the military and his father's experience as both a diplomat and the head of the CIA. His pro-business and pro-energy policies are a product of his family's background as entrepreneurs in the oil industry. His "pull-yourself-up-by-the-bootstraps" social policies are indigenous to the politics of the west Texas plains.

Bush ran in 2000 as a sort of un-Clinton—a straight-shooting, what-you-see-is-what-you-get, man of the people—and he was successful in capturing the anti-Clinton backlash vote: moderates who had tired of the scandals and saw Gore as a continuation of the Clinton regime.

Photo Credit: Paul J. Richards/AFP/Getty Images

George W. Bush waves to his supporters.

But from the beginning, Bush and his administration were polarizing forces—you either loved him or hated him. The controversy that surrounded the 2000 election and the Supreme Court ruling that decided it has come to symbolize the Bush m.o.: We know what we want and we know how to get it.

The Bush platform in 2000 carried many of the themes from his time as governor of Texas to the national stage:

- ✓ Sweeping business and personal income tax cuts
- ✓ Allowing drilling in the Arctic National Wildlife Refuge and other domestic lands
- ✓ The No Child Left Behind education initiative for holding schools accountable through standardized assessment.
- ✓ Enabling faith-based charities to receive federal funding to provide services to the poor
- ✓ Revamping the military to focus on new weapons technology, fewer troops, less international deployment, and more speed and flexibility in tactics

His Record in Office

Bush has been successful in turning his initiatives into law because of Republican control of both houses of Congress. He passed the No Child Left Behind legislation with bi-partisan support, but has since been criticized by many—including John Kerry—who say the law is an unfunded federal mandate that states and local school districts can't afford to implement.

He has enacted three tax cuts, including lower taxes on income from dividends and capital gains. Many argue that the tax cuts have spurred economic recovery from the recession, but others point to the burgeoning national deficit, now the largest in U.S. history, and say that the cuts favor the wealthiest Americans. The Congressional Budget Office estimates that the tax cuts will increase budget deficits by $340 billion if left in place through 2008.

LAUGH TRACK

"Gas prices are up, the stock market is down, Iraq is a mess, and John Kerry is saying, 'How am I gonna beat this guy?"

—David Letterman

Bush added prescription drug coverage to Medicare by enacting the Medicare Act of 2003. Bush supported the Clear Skies Act of 2003, which provides for flexible, market-based incentives for companies to reduce pollution emissions. Under the law, companies can "trade" various types of emissions to stay under a prescribed overall cap. Environmentalists say the act undermines the previous standards imposed by the Clean Air Act.

Bush has been less successful driving legislation on privatizing Social Security, allowing drilling in the Arctic National Wildlife Refuge, and other civil rights legislation, such as a Constitutional amendment banning gay marriages. He has gone against the grain on certain civil rights issues, backing the Supreme Court's ruling upholding the selection of college applicants based on race to improve campus diversity.

Axis of Evil

Bush announced that Iraq would be the next front in the war on terror during his 2002 State of the Union address, proclaiming that Iraq, Iran, and North Korea constituted an "Axis of Evil." Throughout 2002 he pursued a course of diplomatic coercion aimed at getting Saddam Hussein to come clean about Iraq's efforts to produce weapons of mass destruction. When U.N. weapons inspectors failed to get full cooperation, he urged the U.N. to support a U.S.-led invasion of Iraq with the stated goal of ousting Saddam and uncovering the alleged weapons programs.

Bush has had a history of foreign policy unilateralism, including backing out of the Kyoto Protocol on carbon dioxide pollution and doing away with the 1972 Anti-Ballistic Missile Treaty. Members of the U.N. and its Security Council, notably France and Russia, declined to support the use of force in Iraq, but Bush decided to go ahead anyway, in the face of public opposition both at home and abroad. Instead of securing U.N. support, Bush built a "coalition of the willing" to stand behind an invasion of Iraq.

Continued insurgent and terrorist attacks in Iraq, the gruesome spectacle of murdered and mutilated U.S. civilians, plus the disgrace of the Abu Ghraib prison scandal have combined to produce a public relations nightmare and military/foreign relations debacle that may end up backfiring on Bush, who is running his re-election campaign as a war president.

MEET THE NEW BOSS...SAME AS THE OLD BOSS

Was war in Iraq inevitable from the moment George W. Bush took office, a follow-on to the Gulf War to complete the job of ousting Saddam Hussein? George W. Bush's cabinet has a web of ties to previous Republican administrations, especially the foreign policy team.

Colin Powell, Dick Cheney, Paul Wolfowitz, and Condoleeza Rice all worked for George Sr. during Desert Storm in 1991. Wolfowitz, Donald Rumsfeld, Cheney, William Bennett, and Jeb Bush were all charter members of an organization called Project for the New American Century (PNAC), a conservative group whose goal is to promote American foreign policy leadership abroad. From the PNAC's inception, the group issued a number of policy statements that included regime change in Iraq.

The headlong, unilateral way in which the invasion of Iraq was undertaken, the intelligence gaps on the premise of finding weapons of mass destruction, and the connections to the previous Bush administration have led critics to question how much influence George W.'s father has over the current administration and its agenda.

Photo Credit: Stephen Jaffe/AFP/Getty Images

George W. Bush addresses the nation from the deck of the nuclear aircraft carrier USS Abraham Lincoln, May 2003. Bush defended the speech one year later, saying U.S. forces accomplished what they set out to do in Iraq.

Where He Stands on the Issues

Observers of the Bush administration—conservatives and liberals alike—have noted that there has been a dearth of new policy initiatives in the two-plus years since 9/11. The last major policy initiative Bush signed was the Jobs and Growth Tax Relief Reconciliation Act (the full name for the Bush tax cut legislation), which became law in May 2003. This is partly a result of Bush's 2000 campaign initiatives either being passed into law or stalled.

The focus required to carry out the anti-terrorism effort at home and the war effort in Iraq, combined with the replacement of several veteran White House staff members who have resigned with less-experienced successors, has created a new policy slow-down within the administration.

Among the policy initiatives President Bush proposes for a second term, several are continuations of plans he has been working on since 2000. Here's a detailed look at the Bush agenda for a second term.

For a complete summary of George W. Bush's position on all the key issues, see Chapter 11, "Candidate Comparison Guide," p. 157.

Iraq Withdrawal

Although Bush initially opposed U.N. involvement in Iraq during the transition to Iraqi rule, Bush has sought and received the support of a U.N. resolution backing the transition to a new interim government, a slow U.S. troop withdrawal through 2006, and elections in January 2005.

Foreign Policy Beyond Iraq

Bush's stated foreign policy strategy is based on three pillars:

- ✓ Defending the peace by opposing and preventing violence by terrorists and outlaw regimes
- ✓ Preserving the peace by fostering an era of good relations among the world's great powers
- ✓ Extending the peace by seeking to extend the benefits of freedom and prosperity across the globe

This strategy provides the outline for an aggressive, pre-emptive foreign policy, which includes increasing the defense budget by $15.3 billion to more than $379 billion while transforming the military to focus on terrorist threats.

Bush has established pre-emptive strikes as the basis for U.S. foreign policy, and he states that this policy is necessary to prevent terror attacks on the U.S.

Bush's foreign policy strategy focuses on

- ✓ Strengthening the military through better training, housing, and pay for our armed forces. Bush's plan also calls for building up our intelligence services through increases of nearly $3 billion in intelligence budgets.
- ✓ Transforming the military through funding of next-generation weapons such as unmanned aerial vehicles and underwater vehicles, improved infantry communication, small precision bombs, bunker-defeating munitions, and space-based surveillance systems.
- ✓ Developing a strategic missile defense system to protect all armed forces abroad as well as the American homeland. Bush withdrew from the Anti-Ballistic Missile Treaty with Russia in December 2001 to pave the way for developing this program. Bush's 2004 budget provides for more than $9 billion to start work on deploying long-range missile interceptors over the next two years.
- ✓ Advancing his road map for Middle East peace, which calls for creating a Palestinian state and demands democratic reforms within the Palestinian Authority. Bush says Israel must freeze settlement construction, dismantle unauthorized outposts, and not set up walls or fences that would prejudice final negotiations.
- ✓ Increasing the number of U.S. troops in Iraq and widening the Army's "stop-loss" program, which prevents thousands of soldiers in Afghanistan and Iraq from retiring or otherwise leaving the military prior to completing their deployment in combat zones. Bush has not called for an increase in the total number of U.S. troops in the military.

The Economy

Bush's economic plan centers around continuing the tax cuts that he successfully put in place in the past three years. Bush says these tax cuts have been instrumental in pulling the nation out of recession by creating investment opportunities for businesses and stimulating growth by helping Americans keep more of their own money to spend, save, and invest.

Bush wants to make some parts of his tax cuts permanent, including the increase in the child tax credit, elimination of the estate tax, and the new tax incentives for small business investment.

Bush also focuses on creating a free-trade environment for business growth and ending export subsidies for agriculture. He supports expanding NAFTA to include all of the Western Hemisphere, but imposed tariffs that violated WTO rules on foreign steel. Bush lifted the steel tariffs after threats of retaliation from U.S. trading partners.

Bush's economic agenda includes

- ✓ Privatization of Social Security, enabling individuals to voluntarily invest a portion of their Social Security taxes into personal retirement accounts. Bush's plan to strengthen Social Security includes support for Individual Development Accounts—tax-free savings matches for low-income Americans, tax relief, voluntary investment of Social Security taxes in personal retirement accounts, and minimizing risk for workers by allowing them to sell company stock and diversify into other investment options. Bush's plan also calls for allowing "catch up" retirement plan contributions for women who took time off work to raise children, as well as creating property rights in personal retirement accounts for divorced women and expanded benefits for widows.
- ✓ Cutting the budget deficit in half within five years by keeping the Bush tax cuts in place and holding the line on spending.
- ✓ Reducing the lawsuit burden on the economy through tort reform that allows more class action lawsuits and mass tort lawsuits to be moved to federal court. Bush's proposed reforms would also ensure that more settlement dollars go to the injured rather than the trial lawyers.

- ✓ Streamlining regulations and reporting requirements for business. Bush's tax cut plan streamlined tax reporting requirements for small businesses, and he seeks to eliminate well-intentioned compliance regulations that have the unintended effect of killing jobs.

The Environment

Bush has strong ties to the energy industry that have prompted many environmentalists to criticize his environmental policies, most notably his efforts to allow oil companies to drill in the Alaska National Wildlife Refuge.

In keeping with his market-orientated policies, Bush has proposed energy and environment legislation that relies on free market forces to propel business and industry compliance.

Bush's energy and environment policies include

- ✓ Spending $1.2 billion on developing hydrogen fuel to stop dependence on foreign oil. Bush's goal is to produce hydrogen-fuel cell vehicles for use by 2020.
- ✓ Reducing power plant emissions by 70% through his proposed Clear Skies initiative. According to Bush, this plan will save consumers $1 billion annually through reduced business compliance costs.
- ✓ Restoring forests to a natural, fire-resistant condition through his Healthy Forests initiative. This plan calls for looser regulations on forest clearing in federal lands. The Clear Skies and Healthy Forests initiatives are controversial plans that many environmental organizations have criticized as being favorable to industry.
- ✓ Spending $4.4 billion for climate change research and $500 million in tax incentives to improve energy efficiency and promote renewable energy.
- ✓ Proposing a comprehensive national energy plan that includes upgrading the nation's electrical grid, promoting energy efficiency, increasing domestic energy production, and providing enhanced conservation efforts.

Social Issues

Bush's stand on social issues such as abortion and gay marriage has been in keeping with his born-again Christian faith. He characterizes his social policy as "morally traditional and socially inclusive."

Bush opposes abortion except in cases of life-threatening risk, incest, and rape, and he signed the Partial-Birth Abortion Act of 2003. Bush accepts FDA approval of the RU-486 "abortion pill," but is concerned that it will promote more abortions. He has blocked funds to international groups that offer abortion counseling, and he says taxpayer funds shouldn't be used to pay for abortions or abortion counseling.

He has been vocal in calling for a Constitutional amendment defining marriage as between a man and a woman. Bush says states should be able to define their own alternative legal arrangements other than marriage within the Constitutional amendment.

Bush opposes quotas and affirmative action, maintaining that quotas don't work and they "pit people against each other." Instead, Bush supports what he calls "affirmative access," guaranteeing admittance to a university if you're in the top 10% of a high school graduating class. He wants to enhance access to the middle class by "challenging the soft bigotry of low expectations."

Bush wants to renew key aspects of the Patriot Act set to expire in 2005. The Patriot Act was developed by the Bush administration in response to the 9/11 attacks, and he supports the increased information-gathering techniques the Act allows. Bush supports the policy of labeling U.S. citizens "enemy combatants" if they are involved in terrorist activities.

ACTS OF FAITH

How important are the candidates' religious beliefs to voters in this year's campaign?

Judging by a Time magazine poll, the correlation between voters' religious beliefs and the candidates they support is strong. In the Time poll, voters who characterized themselves as "very religious" support Bush over Kerry 59% to 35%. Those who characterized themselves as "not religious" support Kerry 69% to 22%.

Neither Kerry nor Bush has hesitated to practice their respective religions on the campaign trail. The difference is that Bush has not been shy about stating that God has an impact on how he makes his decisions in the Oval Office. Bush told Bob Woodward that he didn't need to consult his father, the former president, about going to war in Iraq because he was consulting "a higher father."

This strong reliance on faith attracts some voters to Bush and scares others—not surprisingly, the split falls along party lines. The Time magazine poll indicated that 70% of Republicans say a president should be guided by his faith when making policy, while 63% of Democrats said he should not.

Bush supporters see his faith as a major reason to vote for him. His social platform aligns well with conservative religious beliefs. Bush's critics site his statements about faith guiding his policy as a sign that he is closed off to outside opinions—even those of his own cabinet members. Bush's faith is one of the most divisive elements of his presidency, and it will continue to polarize voters right up to election day.

Gun Control

Bush favors enforcing existing laws more aggressively, including the ban on automatic weapons. He says we need to keep guns out of the hands of the wrong people, and supports instant background checks (as opposed to three-day waiting periods) at gun shows and gun shops. Bush supports voluntary—not mandatory—trigger locks and says government should fund a program to distribute trigger locks to the public. He also supports raising the minimum age for juveniles to carry guns. In keeping with his tort reform agenda, Bush wants to restrict lawsuits against gun makers.

Crime and the Death Penalty

Bush supports the death penalty because he believes it deters crime. He says DNA evidence should be used to assure guilt before execution, and says death penalty clemency should be used in cases of unfair legal process or where the defendant has been proved innocent, not for repentant criminals.

Bush's law enforcement agenda focuses on homeland security: protecting the nation against terrorist threats. His homeland security agenda includes creation of the Terrorist Threat Integration Center, several laws tightening immigration and border security, and reorganizing law enforcement agencies such as the FBI to better focus on terrorist activities.

Bush launched the Department of Homeland Security and has proposed an additional $3.6 billion for terrorist preparedness funds in 2005 to help local law enforcement agencies and first responders prepare for terrorist attacks.

Health Care

Bush has made modernizing Medicare a priority for his agenda if he were to win a second term. He wants to commit up to $400 billion to modernize Medicare over the next 10 years. Bush's plan would give all Medicare beneficiaries access to prescription drug coverage without government dictating drug choice.

The plan would give Medicare beneficiaries their choice of individual health care plans, choice of doctor and treatment location, as well as full coverage for disease prevention such as screenings for cancer, diabetes, and osteoporosis.

Bush wants to implement medical liability tort reform to reduce health care costs. He supports passing a Patients' Bill of Rights that says doctors should decide what treatment patients receive, not insurance companies.

Other Key Initiatives in Bush's Agenda

Beyond the positions already covered, Bush has several other key initiatives he proposes as part of his policy agenda.

Bush wants to provide increased funding for schools to help them implement the mandates of his No Child Left Behind education program. He will continue pursuing school vouchers that allow parents to send their children to private schools instead of public schools, and he will seek more funding for foreign aid programs and drug abuse treatment programs.

Another key initiative for Bush is to continue seeking government funding for faith-based aid programs and charitable organizations.

Bush will continue to focus on national security, tax cuts, tort reform, and defense spending, building on his policy agenda from his first term in office.

You can see Bush's complete campaign agenda at **www.georgewbush.com**.

9

"John would clearly say, 'If I could make my dream come true, it would be running for president of the Untied States.' It was not a casual interest. It was a serious, stated interest. His lifetime ambition was to be in political office."

—William Stanberry, John Kerry's debate team partner at Yale

John Kerry: Political Prodigy

If George W. Bush is the prodigal son who reluctantly and somewhat haphazardly followed in his father's footsteps all the way to the Oval Office, John F. Kerry is the political prodigy who has seemingly been rehearsing, scheming, and dreaming for his chance to become president ever since he was a callow prep school kid.

Kerry knew early on that he wanted to be a politician—it seemed inevitable to his friends and classmates. He had the looks, the bearing, and the intellect for it. He had the Boston Brahmin ancestors, the prep school and Ivy League education, and the Kennedy-esque accent. He even had the right initials: JFK.

But from the beginning, Kerry's earnestness about politics set him up as an easy target: His classmates at Yale thought he was aloof and haughty—a perception that has followed him to the present day—and maybe a bit too full of himself. Some of his classmates at Yale joked that JFK stood for "Just For Kerry."

LAUGH TRACK

"This is so weird. I saw the new John Kerry campaign commercial and he says, "I'm John Kerry and I approve of this message—if I have one."

—Craig Kilborn

Out in Left Field, or More Toward the Center?

One of the Bush campaign's attack ads on John Kerry says, "Kerry's problem is not that people don't know him. It's that people do."

But how much do you *really* know about John Kerry? That's the problem every challenger faces, especially John Kerry in this year's war-time election: getting air time versus the president, the commander in chief, to help explain who Candidate Kerry is and what he stands for.

The Bush campaign has done a good job of defining Kerry in the aftermath of the Democratic primaries as a "flip-flopper" on the issues and a classic tax-and-spend liberal. But how true are these claims?

Are Kerry's positions more centrist than the ads would have you believe?

Did Kerry really waffle on support for the Iraq war and the Patriot Act? And if so, is that a black mark against him, or a sign of intelligent and nuanced leadership?

Kerry's Senate Career

Kerry's voting record as a Senator is extensive—he has served on Capitol Hill since 1984—but he decided early on that he would make his name in the Senate as an investigator rather than a legislator. This grew out of his background as a district attorney as well as his desire to make a reputation separate from his fellow Senator from Massachusetts, Ted Kennedy, the king of Senate lawmakers. In 1986, Kerry led the Senate investigation into the Iran-Contra affair, which linked U.S. weapons sales to Iran and CIA drug money with funding of the anti-communist Contra rebels in Nicaragua.

Kerry also led the initiative to normalize relations with Vietnam by teaming up with Republican Senator John McCain, another Vietnam vet, to investigate reports of prisoners of war still being held in Vietnam. Together, Kerry and McCain resolved the POW issue and, in many ways, closed the circle on Kerry's—and the nation's—Vietnam experience.

Kerry's close ties with McCain have led to speculation that he would name McCain as his vice presidential nominee in a move to garner crossover votes from moderate Republicans. McCain mounted a strong challenge to Bush's campaign during the 2000 Republican primaries.

John Kerry on the campaign trail.

JOHN FORBES KERRY—FACT FILE

United States Senator from Massachusetts.

Born: December 11, 1943, Denver, Colorado.

Education: Yale (B.A., 1966), Boston College (J.D., law degree, 1976).

Religion: Roman Catholic.

Marriage: To first wife, Julia Thorne in 1970. Divorced 1988. To second wife, Teresa Simoes-Ferreira Heinz, May 26, 1995.

Children: Alexandra Kerry (1973), Vanessa Kerry (1976); Stepsons: John Heinz Jr., Andre Heinz, Christopher Heinz.

Career: District Attorney, public official.

Political Party: Democrat.

Writings: *The New War: The Web of Crime that Threatens America's Security* (1997), and *A Call to Service: My Vision for a Better America* (2003).

Pets: Yellow canary named Sunshine.

Hobbies: Skiing, windsurfing, snowboarding, playing hockey, playing acoustic guitar, riding a Harley.

The Most Liberal Senator

Despite Kerry's protests that "labels are so silly in American politics," the Bush campaign has been able to make the "tax-and-spend liberal" tag stick with Kerry. The prime piece of evidence on display is the annual congressional vote ratings published by *National Journal,* the weekly magazine of Washington politics and policy.

Every year, the *National Journal* ranks senators and congressmen on liberal and conservative scales of 0 to 100 for their votes on economic policy, social policy, and foreign policy. Kerry's composite liberal score for 2003 was 96.5 out of a possible 100—the highest liberal score in the Senate.

Kerry's score puts him to the left of Ted Kennedy (88.3) and other noted liberal senators such as Paul Sarbanes of Maryland (94.7) and Barbara Boxer of California (91.2).

Kerry has been named the *Journal*'s top liberal three other times in his twenty years in the Senate: 1986, 1988, and 1990, and Kerry has consistently placed among the most liberal senators. Kerry had a perfect 100 liberal rating on social issues 10 out of 18 years he was scored.

Photo by Terry Ashe/Time Life Pictures/Getty Images.

John Kerry being sworn in for his first term as senator by George H.W. Bush, 1985.

Where He Stands on the Issues

Summing up Kerry's voting record in a liberal versus conservative ranking gives you a good idea of his political leanings, but it doesn't provide the full picture of his complex track record in office. Over the course of nearly 20 years as a Senator, Kerry has voted more than 6,500 times and sponsored more than 370 bills. Let's take a look at the positions he has taken on the major issues.

For a complete summary of John Kerry's position on all the key issues, see Chapter 11, "Candidate Comparison Guide," **p.157**.

Strong Interest in Foreign Policy

Although Kerry is hardly a law-making machine (only nine of the bills he sponsored have become law), his work on the Iran-Contra and Vietnam POW investigations, and the fact that he turned down a spot on the powerful Senate Appropriations Committee (which controls funding legislation) for a spot on the Foreign Relations Committee show that foreign affairs have always been important to Kerry.

Kerry spent his childhood living in Berlin, Oslo, and Switzerland as the son of a State Department diplomat. This combined with his war experience in Vietnam has shaped Kerry's views on foreign policy—his preference for dealing with problems overseas through diplomatic engagement rather than intervention.

Still, Kerry's stance on Iraq has proven difficult for him to defend. He voted yes on authorizing Bush to use force in Iraq, but he later voted against the $87 billion supplemental funding bill to provide financing for the war effort. Bush has used Kerry's own words against him in one of his ads: "I actually did vote for the $87 billion before I voted against it."

Kerry defends his votes by saying that he voted for the initial authorization to use force as a way to put muscle behind enforcing U.N. resolutions. As with other Bush initiatives Kerry has voted for, Kerry says Bush failed in his implementation of the policy, invading Iraq without U.N. approval and without the support of key allies.

LAUGH TRACK

"John Kerry will undergo surgery to repair his right shoulder. He originally hurt it when he suddenly switched positions on Iraq."

—Craig Kilborn

Sending a Message on Iraq

Kerry and other senators, including eight Republicans, tried to make $10 billion of the reconstruction money in Iraq and Afghanistan a loan that would be repaid. Bush threatened to veto the bill if it included the loan provision.

After the vote, Kerry said, "The best way to support our troops and take the target off their backs is with a real strategy to win the peace in Iraq—not by throwing $87 billion at George Bush's failed policies. I am voting no on the Iraq resolution to hold the president accountable and force him to finally develop a real plan that secures the safety of our troops and stabilizes Iraq."

Kerry also tried to tie the war financing bill to a repeal of the Bush tax cuts, saying, "Rather than asking for shared sacrifice from Americans...[Bush] has refused to repeal any of his tax cuts for the wealthy to pay for rebuilding Iraq."

Kerry's plan for postwar Iraq includes turning over administration to the U.N., led by Lakhdar Brahimi—a plan Bush has adopted—launching a training effort to rebuild Iraqi security forces, and involving NATO in the ongoing security mission.

Before this war, Kerry voted in favor of several lesser military actions that took place during the Bush, Clinton, Bush Sr., and Reagan administrations, including Afghanistan in 2001, Bosnia in 1999, Somalia in 1992, Panama in 1989, and Grenada in 1983. Kerry voted against the first Iraq invasion—the Gulf War in 1991, but he says he won't hesitate to use force to fight terror.

★ *WHAT HE SAYS:*
"We may well have to use force to fight terrorism. I will not hesitate to do so. But if I am president, the United States will never go to war because we want to. We will only go to war because we have to." —John Kerry

★ *WHAT HE WANTS YOU TO HEAR:*
I'm strong on defense and the war on terrorism, but I won't get us into a quagmire like Vietnam—or Iraq.

★ *BUT DON'T FORGET:*
Kerry initially voted for the Iraq war before voting against the supplemental funding bill that followed.

PLAYING THE ABU GHRAIB CARD

The Abu Ghraib prison abuse scandal in Iraq may turn out to be the largest election-year political football ever dropped in a challenger's lap. John Kerry has shown no hesitation to use the scandal in his campaign tactics.

Along with other members of Congress, Kerry called for Defense Secretary Donald Rumsfeld's resignation, which Bush denied. He referred to the abuse scandal regularly in his campaign speeches. The Kerry campaign also sent out a mass fundraising e-mail calling for Rumsfeld's resignation.

"Keep the ball rolling!" said the message from Mary Beth Cahill, Kerry's campaign manager. "Donate now!

"Over the past week we have all been shocked by the pictures from the Abu Ghraib prison in Iraq. John Kerry has called on Donald Rumsfeld to resign, and today we're asking you to support him by adding your name to the call for Rumsfeld to resign."

If you received the e-mail, you could add your name to the electronic petition and also donate cash online.

Kerry's speeches have stayed on point: "The chain of command goes all the way to the Oval Office. America does not merely need a new secretary of defense. We need a new president."

The Abu Ghraib photos have provided powerful ammunition for the Kerry campaign, dropping President Bush's approval rating to all-time lows. But many Democrats are wondering why Kerry has not played up the issue to greater advantage.

One reason for Kerry to tread carefully is the desire not to be seen as undermining the efforts of U.S. troops in Iraq. Another reason could be Kerry's own history as a whistleblower for violations of the Geneva Convention in Vietnam.

As a leader of Vietnam Veterans Against the War, Kerry created a stir when he testified against the war before the Senate Foreign Relations Committee in 1971, claiming that U.S. soldiers had committed war crimes:

"They personally raped, cut off ears, cut off heads, taped wires from portable telephones to human genitals and turned up the power, cut off limbs, blew up bodies, randomly shot civilians, razed villages, shot cattle and dogs for fun, poisoned food stocks, and generally ravaged the countryside of South Vietnam," Kerry said, in his infamous testimony.

For the Kerry campaign, this link to the war protest movement may not be the image they want voters to have in mind when they think about electing a new commander in chief. You can look at it in one of two ways: Either Kerry was undermining the efforts of his fighting comrades in Vietnam by repeating hearsay, or Kerry was a principled objector to violations of the Geneva Convention and a poorly-run war without a purpose.

Kerry has summed up his views on Abu Ghraib by saying he would take full responsibility for any such actions. "When I am president," Kerry said, "I will demand accountability from those who serve, and I will take responsibility for their actions."

Photo courtesy Kerry Campaign via Getty Images.

John Kerry with the crew of his swift boat, Vietnam.

Progressive Internationalism

Beyond Iraq, Kerry advocates a foreign policy of "progressive internationalism," as opposed to what he calls Bush's "erratic unilateralism." Kerry's policy vision is to "engage diplomatically in creating alliances that enhance collective security." Kerry says that "America's safety depends on rallying the forces of freedom. Engagement to shape a safer world is the urgent imperative of our time."

Kerry's foreign policy priorities include

- ✓ Securing Afghanistan with a lasting peace so that the conditions that gave rise to the terrorist threats cannot take hold there again.
- ✓ Securing peace in the Middle East through active support of Israel, which he calls "our most important ally," and establishment of a viable Palestinian state. Kerry supports the Bush administration roadmap as an acceptable approach to pursuing Mid-East peace, but says the initiative was long overdue and that Bush neglect of the Israeli-Palestinian conflict has aggravated the terrorist threat. Kerry says the U.S. must take a more active role to bring both sides together, with the support of European and Arab allies.
- ✓ Supporting the military through updated equipment and tactics that are better suited to modern warfare, including better intelligence, advanced communications, long-range airpower, and highly mobile ground forces. Kerry also supports improving health care, housing, and wages for military personnel.
- ✓ Promoting democracy and respect for human rights through support of democratic regimes around the world. Kerry sponsored the Code of Conduct of Arms Transfers Act, which would prohibit U.S. military aid to nations that are undemocratic, do not adequately protect human rights, or attack other nations. However, Kerry voted to kill an amendment that would require sanctions on other countries if they were found to be selling illicit weapons of mass destruction. He also voted yes on granting permanent normal trade relations with China, regardless of human rights violations.
- ✓ Fighting the HIV/AIDS epidemic through increased aid to nations hardest hit by the disease. Kerry wrote major portions of the AIDS and Tuberculosis Relief Act, which was passed by Congress in 2000.

- ✓ Supporting arms control and non-proliferation measures that will help secure nuclear weapons and materials that can be used to make weapons of mass destruction. Kerry fought Bush's withdrawal from the Comprehensive Nuclear Test Ban Treaty.
- ✓ Increasing efforts to develop alternative energy sources, which will help reduce dependence on foreign oil, specifically from the Middle East. Kerry's plan includes creating an "Energy Security and Conservation Trust" that will fund efforts to bring alternative energy sources such as hydrogen power into the mainstream. Funds for the energy plan will come from existing oil and gas royalties from federal lands.

The Economy

In many ways, Kerry has taken positions on jobs and the economy that fit with his identity as a dyed-in-the-wool liberal: He has favored higher gas taxes as a way to reduce fuel consumption and he has favored increasing the minimum wage. He voted against all of Bush's tax cut legislation.

But Kerry has taken some surprisingly conservative positions on economic issues as well—probably more so in this area of his policy than in any other.

Kerry was in favor of NAFTA, the North American Free Trade Agreement, which opened up the move of many U.S. jobs to Mexico, while also favoring tax incentives to businesses that keep jobs in the U.S. He has proposed education reforms that rankle the powerful teacher's unions by trading increased pay for performance-based job ratings.

LAUGH TRACK

"They had a profile of John Kerry on the news and they said his first wife was worth around $300 million and his second wife, his current wife, is worth around $700 million. So when John Kerry says he's going after the wealthy in this country, he's not just talking. He's doing it!"

—Jay Leno

He hooked up with John McCain to fight for keeping the Internet as a tax-free zone, and he has supported cutting taxes on capital gains and stock dividends. He also has been a vocal supporter of federal deficit-reduction legislation, leading the way with conservative Democrat Fritz Hollings to pass the Gramm-Rudman-Hollings balanced-budget law.

Kerry's economic priorities include

- ✓ Keeping what Kerry calls "middle class tax cuts." He wants to protect increases in the child tax credit, the reduced marriage tax penalty, and the new tax bracket that helps people save $350 on their first level of income. He proposes more tax credits for health care and college tuition.
- ✓ Investing in manufacturing jobs through tax credits for companies that create goods and keep jobs in the U.S. He also favors enforcing fair trade laws with our trading partners, as well as investment in research and development, jobs training, and facilities improvement.
- ✓ Focusing on creating jobs through better education, including full funding of the No Child Left Behind legislation, a fund for state education budgets, and a tax credit for college tuition.
- ✓ Closing corporate tax loopholes by going after companies that bank in foreign countries. Kerry also wants to raise investor confidence and protect retirement savings by ensuring strong enforcement of corporate governance laws by the Security and Exchange Commission.
- ✓ Protecting workers through improved workplace health, safety, and overtime regulations. He also favors increasing the minimum wage and indexing it to inflation.

The Environment

Protecting the environment has been one of the consistent themes of Kerry's political career. Two of the bills Kerry sponsored protect fisheries and promote marine biology research. He opposed Bush's withdrawal of support for the Kyoto global warming accords and he has worked with John McCain in an effort to raise average fuel economy standards to 36 miles per gallon.

Kerry was a leader of Democratic opposition to Bush's plan to drill for oil in Alaska's Arctic National Wildlife Refuge. He voted against confirming Gale Norton as secretary of the interior in 2001. Norton is an advocate of market-oriented environmental policies, including outsourcing of some National Parks Service jobs to private firms.

Kerry has also opposed proposed rollbacks to the Corporate Average Fuel Economy (CAFE) fuel efficiency standards and reducing funds for renewable and solar energy research.

Kerry's environmental policies include

- ✓ Inventing our way out of foreign-oil dependency instead of drilling our way out. This means development of alternative energy sources such as hydrogen and improving energy efficiency in homes, schools, and businesses, and developing renewable sources of electricity.
- ✓ Entering a "Conservation Covenant" to protect and "tread lightly" on federal lands. This would require energy and mineral royalties from public lands to be reinvested into protecting the land.
- ✓ Promoting a domestic trading system to reduce greenhouse gasses by 10% by 2010 and shifting environmental problem-solving from federal to local government without lowering federal standards.
- ✓ Promoting "Clean and Green Communities" by coordinating efforts to reduce urban sprawl and traffic congestion. This includes ending federal regulations and tax incentives that encourage sprawl and coordinating these initiatives with federal housing and transportation policies—buying and investing in older homes and using transportation dollars for improved public transportation systems such as light rail, streetcars, and pedestrian-friendly cities.

Social Issues

If the hot-button social issue is abortion, John Kerry is certainly in line with the standard liberal position: He is adamantly pro-choice in all circumstances, including voting no on Bush's bill to ban partial-birth abortions. He has said that he will not nominate a Supreme Court justice who won't uphold *Roe v. Wade*. But he has shown some more centrist leanings (or, as some might say, wafflings) on other social issues.

He voted for the Patriot Act and supported roving wiretaps even before 9/11. He wants to "mend, not end" affirmative action, by shifting emphasis from group preferences to economic empowerment for all disadvantaged citizens. He signed the "New Agenda for a New Decade" manifesto, which says "we should resist an 'identity politics' that confers rights and entitlements on groups, and instead affirm our common rights and responsibilities as citizens."

Kerry voted no on the Defense of Marriage Act (DOMA), which would have prohibited same-sex marriage and he says he would oppose a Constitutional amendment banning gay marriage, but he also states that he believes marriage should be between a man and a woman. He has stated that he does not support the Massachusetts law allowing gay marriage in that state, but he believes marriage law should be left to individual states.

WHAT IF?—CATHOLICS FOR KERRY?

Catholics make up the single largest religious voting block in the United States, comprising more than 26% of registered voters. Between 1948 and 1968, Catholics were reliably Democratic, helping carry John F. Kennedy, the nation's first and only Catholic president, into office by supporting him with 83% of the Catholic vote.

Since 1968, however, Catholics have become a bellwether voting block, consistently supporting the winning candidate as a group—whether he was a Republican or Democrat.

Can John Kerry translate his status as a Catholic into a victory in November? He's been successful at winning the important Catholic vote in Massachusetts, where Catholics make up about 50% of the voting population. And he won 62% of the Catholic vote in the Super Tuesday primaries this spring.

But Kerry's political views on several key issues are at odds with the Catholic church, including his positions on abortion and gay marriage. Kerry has been receiving communion at Catholic churches on the campaign trail, and some Catholic leaders have threatened to turn his public policy into an issue for the church.

Kerry's archbishop in Boston, Sean O'Malley, has stated that pro-choice Catholics are in a state of grave sin and thus are not properly taking communion. Another archbishop, Raymond Burke of St. Louis, denied Kerry the opportunity to take communion while Kerry was campaigning in his area.

Will the communion issue hurt Kerry among Catholic voters? Polls show that Catholics are pro-choice and support gay marriage at about the same level as the total voting population. Catholic voters who are themselves at odds with the church over these issues may side with Kerry if church leaders press the communion issue.

As for Kerry, he says, "We have separation of church and state in this country. As John Kennedy said very clearly, I will be a president who happens to be Catholic, not a Catholic president."

Gun Control

Kerry voted with the Coalition to Stop Gun Violence 100% of the time and received an "F" from the NRA for his control votes. He voted for the Brady Bill, which requires a 5-day waiting period and background checks for handgun purchases, and he voted for the Assault Weapons Ban. Kerry touts himself as a gun owner and sportsman (read: hunter) on his campaign Web site, but says that he will fully enforce all gun laws on the books and will close the gun show background check loophole.

Crime and the Death Penalty

Kerry is a former prosecutor who sponsored a "two strikes, you're out" life imprisonment bill for sex offenders, but Kerry is also opposed to the death penalty other than in cases of international and domestic terrorism. He supports a moratorium on federal executions until DNA testing can be used to ensure that all those on death row are guilty.

Photo by Paula Bronstein/Getty Images.

John Kerry attends mass with his wife, Teresa Heinz Kerry.

He voted against limiting death penalty appeals and mandatory prison terms for crimes involving firearms. He voted for increased funding to hire up to 50,000 more police officers in the next five years. And he was an original cosponsor of the Violence Against Women Act, which enhanced federal penalties for acts of domestic violence and provided more than $1 billion for battered women's shelters.

Health Care

Kerry says he will cap catastrophic medical costs for all Americans at $50,000 and reduce premiums for everyone by $1,000. How will he pay for this? As with other Kerry entitlement programs, he says he will leave "middle class" tax cuts in place, but "roll back Bush's tax cut for the wealthiest Americans."

Kerry says health care should be "a right, not a privilege. We must end the disgrace of America being the only industrialized nation on the planet not to make health care accessible to all our citizens." He says he will give every American access to the same plan members of Congress have (the Federal Employees Health Care Benefits Program). He wants to ensure that health care is guaranteed for every child through Medicaid coverage of all children who are within 300% of poverty-level income.

Kerry voted yes on a bill to allow import of prescription drugs from Canada and he voted yes on including prescription drugs in Medicare.

Kerry's Agenda

When Kerry's campaign was flagging in November 2003, he cleaned house and hired Mary Beth Cahill to run his campaign. Cahill's successful resurrection of Kerry's campaign and her ties to Ted Kennedy may be an indication of what Kerry's White House staff and cabinet could look like. Cahill has worked for Emily's List, a political action committee for women's issues, and as chief of staff for Ted Kennedy.

Kerry has spelled out his action plan for his first 100 days in office, outlining his vision and priorities. Here's what he would focus on if he became president:

1. A new National Education Trust Fund to fully fund federal education initiatives.
2. A new era of national service, calling on all Americans to serve in schools, nursing homes, day care centers, and other social institutions and programs.

3. End the "Era of Ashcroft" by naming a new attorney general to focus on protecting women's rights, civil rights, workers' rights, and enforcing anti-trust laws.
4. Repeal the Bush assault on the environment and make the U.S. independent of Middle East oil within 10 years through development of alternative energy sources such as solar energy, hydrogen, ethanol, and wind.
5. Rejoin the community of nations by declaring the Bush policy of unilateralism over and repairing relationships with allies.
6. Undertake a major legislative plan to provide affordable health care for all U.S. citizens.
7. Reward companies that create jobs in the U.S. through health care funding and tax credits, while pursuing criminal penalties for companies that defraud investors and shutting down tax incentives and loopholes for companies that take jobs overseas.
8. Create a middle class economy instead of a privileged class economy by repealing Bush tax cuts for the wealthiest Americans and investing that money in education and health care, protecting middle class tax cuts such as child credits, and eliminating the marriage penalty.
9. Cut the deficit in half in four years by eliminating corporate tax breaks while supporting programs such as Social Security and Medicare.
10. End influence peddling by reinstating the five-year ban on lobbying and requiring any meetings Congress members have with lobbyists be made public.

"Gore beat Gore. He didn't get Tennessee, his home state. That would have made him president. And he blundered in Florida and didn't ask for a statewide recount."

—Ralph Nader

Ralph Nader: Advocate or Spoiler?

"Go ahead, Kerry—just try to get farther to the left on the issues than me. I dare you." That seems to be Ralph Nader's ongoing harangue of John Kerry during this year's campaign—a kind of scolding sermon designed to boost Nader's profile as the true progressive candidate, to gain exposure for the agenda he advances, and perhaps, in the process, to keep Kerry's platform from straying too far from its liberal roots.

Once again, Democrats are concerned by Nader's shadowing of Kerry and the possibility that his presence on the ballot in November could siphon off enough votes to cost them the election in a repeat of 2000. Four years ago, Nader captured nearly three million popular votes and had an impact in several key states, particularly Florida, where his 97,488 votes could have made the difference had they gone to Gore instead of Bush. Nader also pulled in 22,198 in New Hampshire, a state Bush won by 7,211 votes.

A Vote for Bush?

Even if Nader wins only a small portion of what he did in 2000, he could still make an impact on Kerry's chances against Bush, with whom Kerry is locked in a statistical dead heat according to most polls.

Several leading progressive publications and political organizations have asked Nader to bow out of the race in the name of booting Bush out of office. And despite a tense meeting with Nader to talk about coordinating efforts to oust Bush from office, Kerry has said that "a vote for Ralph Nader is a vote for George Bush."

Photo by Craig Mitchelldyer/Getty Images

Ralph Nader speaks to an audience in Portland, OR, as supporters try to gather enough signatures for him to qualify for the Oregon ballot.

RALPH NADER—FACT FILE

Consumer advocate and author

Born: February 27, 1934, Winsted, Connecticut

Education: Princeton University (magna cum laude, B.A., 1955), Harvard University (J.D., 1958)

Marriage: Never married

Children: None

Career: Consumer advocate, author, attorney, public official

Political Party: Independent

Writings: Dozens of books, including *Unsafe at Any Speed* (1965), and his most recent book, *Crashing the Party: Taking on the Corporate Government in an Age of Surrender* (2002)

The Crypto-Republicans

There's little doubt that Nader has a clear agenda behind his campaign. He has always been anti-corporation, and his message to voters is that big business and big government have teamed up in a way that hurts our democracy and hurts the common man. This populist message plays well not only on the left, but with some of the same voters who backed Ross Perot's successful third-party campaigns in 1992 and 1996. In fact, Nader has garnered the endorsement of the Reform Party that Perot founded to help him get on the ballot in seven states, including key battleground states such as Florida and Michigan.

This boosts Nader's claim that he won't just be ripping away votes from the Democrats—he says disenchanted Republicans will be voting for him too. "If the Democrats cannot beat George Bush, that means they're not Democrats; they're Crypto-Republicans. And people will always choose the real thing."

A big part of the Nader message—and the reason he says he won't drop out of the race—is that there is no longer a difference between Democrats and Republicans: Both parties are beholden to the special interests of large, multinational corporations. He says the Bush White House is a front for a large oil company and can point to Kerry's record of receiving millions in financial support from corporations and special interest PACs.

NADER TRADERS AND THE SPOILER EFFECT

With Web sites such as StopNader! and efforts by the Democratic Party to keep Ralph Nader off the ballot, will Nader have the same "spoiler effect" on this year's election as he is alleged to have had in 2000?

Maybe not. There is a chorus of voices coming from the left of the political spectrum urging liberal and progressive voters not to vote for Nader—no matter how much they all may like his positions on the issues—and band together behind John Kerry in an effort to get George Bush out of office.

The editors of *The Nation*, perhaps the leading liberal news magazine, have sent Nader an open letter pleading with him not to run—this from the magazine that published one of his first articles, "The *Safe* Car You Can't Buy," back in 1959. That article was the basis for Nader's best-selling book, *Unsafe at Any Speed.*

A petition from leading leftists such as Noam Chomsky, Angela Davis, and Frances M. Beal declares that "traditional debates on the left about the value of electoral politics and the lesser evil pale in the light of the need to defeat Bush..."

Apparently, Kerry has earned the status of the lesser evil to these folks—the "Anyone But Bush" candidate. And there's a slew of blogs and newspaper columns floating around that ascribe some less-than-noble motives to Nader's campaign: He's running on ego alone. He's running on spite because the Democrats shunned him. He wants to sabotage the Democrats because that's the only way to get the parties to diverge.

But the question remains—will those who voted for Nader in 2000 "make their vote count" by throwing it to Kerry this time? A number of Nader supporters in key battleground states say they will trade votes with friends in non-battleground states—the so-called Nader Trader strategy—to make sure they don't hurt Kerry's chances of defeating Bush.

Others are angry that their vote for Nader puts them in the role of spoilers. "More than 49% of eligible voters didn't vote," says Benjamin Beatty, a Nader supporter. "How come they're not considered spoilers?"

As for Nader, he maintains that the two-party-dominated Electoral College system means he probably lost more votes to Gore last time than the other way around. He's advocating changes to our electoral system that include Instant Runoff Voting (IRV) and proportional representation systems that would give candidates from other parties a fighting chance.

An initiative from the Center for Voting and Democracy, Instant Runoff Voting is a voting system that ensures a winning candidate will receive an absolute majority of the votes cast. It's a system that could be used as a popular vote alternative to the Electoral College in Presidential elections.

IRV enables voters to rank all candidates when they vote. The votes are then counted at one time in a simulation of run-off elections. On the first count, only first-choice votes are tallied. If none of the candidates wins a majority on the first count, the last place candidate is eliminated and the next-choice votes from the eliminated candidate are distributed to the rest of the field. The process is repeated until a majority winner emerges.

IRV prevents spoiler candidates from throwing an election result and provides a more representative picture of voter opinions. In the case of the 2000 election, Nader votes likely would have gone to elect Gore. In 1992 and possibly 1996, Perot votes would have gone to elect either Bush or Dole instead of Clinton.

To learn more about IRV, go to **http://www.fairvote.org/irv/**.

Photo by Craig Mitchelldyer/Getty Images.

A protestor urges voters not to vote for Nader.

Beyond November

Nader maintains that he must stay in the race as a way of keeping the Democrats true to the left—and he sees this as more of a political movement than a campaign. "This goes way beyond November," Nader says. "This is a movement that has to proliferate in all directions, year after year."

For their part, the Democrats want to keep Nader off the ballot in as many states as possible, especially the key battleground states. By getting on the ballot in states like Wisconsin and Ohio, Nader could keep Kerry from moving too far to the center to attract swing voters.

But Nader suggests that his presence in the campaign can help Kerry by presenting a sharp contrast to the Bush policies he says have failed, in particular, the war in Iraq. Nader has established himself as the hardcore anti-war candidate, calling for a complete withdrawal of U.S. troops in six months, while Bush and Kerry have, in general, both converged on a policy of staying the course and involving the U.N. more.

Controlling the Power of Economic Interests

For those who question Nader's motives for running, he responds by saying that his campaign is simply a natural platform for his consumer advocacy. Nader launched his public career with his 1965 book *Unsafe at Any Speed,* which claimed many American cars were unsafe because of structural design flaws, especially the sporty Corvair, produced by General Motors.

Nader's consumer rights mission is summed up in the book, when he says, "A great problem of contemporary life is how to control the power of economic interests which ignore the harmful effects of their applied science and technology."

Nader's groundbreaking book and the lawsuit that followed it prompted auto makers to pursue stronger crash testing and driver safety when designing their cars. Since then, Nader has written dozens of books, many of which have resulted in government regulatory agencies, consumer safety laws, and consumer advocacy groups such as Public Citizen, Buyers Up, the Public Interest Research Group (PIRG), Congress Watch, and Tax Reform Research Group.

LAUGH TRACK

"John Kerry and Ralph Nader met face to face; it was a historic meeting. Astronomers said today their meeting actually created what is called a 'charisma black hole.'"

—Jay Leno

The work of Nader's groups is credited with investigating citizen issues ranging from corruption in Congress to health, environmental, and economic concerns. Nader's groups have helped pass numerous laws and establish federal agencies, including the Freedom of Information Act, the Safe Drinking Water Act, the Occupational Safety and Health Administration (OSHA), and the Consumer Product Safety Administration. A brief list of books he has published includes

Who Runs Congress?
Vanishing Air (air pollution)
The Chemical Feast (food industry regulation)
Collision Course (air travel safety)
The Big Boys (corporate executive corruption)

Where He Stands on the Issues

The common theme in Nader's writing and advocacy groups is greater accountability for big business and limiting the influence of corporations in government. He's opposed to concentration of power and moneyed interests and wants to expand the agenda to the voter, worker, consumer, and shareholder.

According to the Nader campaign, his agenda is summed up by three themes:

- ✓ "Freedom from Fear—This election is dominated by fear: The Republicans play on the fear of terrorism and the Democrats play on the fear of Bush. One of the goals of this campaign is to free voters from fear so they can vote their conscience, their interests, and their dreams."
- ✓ "Shift the Power—Washington, DC is corporate-occupied territory. This prevents putting in place policies that can improve the lives of Americans: health care for all, a living wage, ending poverty, and fair taxes."
- ✓ "Solution Revolution—There are many solutions to our common problems, more solutions than we deploy. The Nader Campaign will highlight the solutions to our everyday problems in order to create a culture and society that serves our living standards and our just needs."

The last theme puts the objectives of the Nader presidential campaign in perspective. The presidential bid provides Nader with a platform to advance his reform agenda on the biggest possible political stage. He's not trying to win an election; he's trying to create a movement. And because he views Washington politics—both Democratic and Republican—as dominated by corporate influence, the only way he feels he can make an impact is to run for office.

But because he knows he has virtually no chance of getting elected, his positions on the issues can sometimes be viewed as impractical or extreme. In many cases, his positions are kind of like the beauty pageant contestant saying, "I wish for world peace." We may agree with the objective, but how do we accomplish it?

For a complete summary of Ralph Nader's position on all the key issues, see Chapter 11, "Candidate Comparison Guide" on **page 157**.

According to Nader, even if he doesn't have a chance to win, the fact that he can get his views and ideas into the public eye means they are more likely to be adopted by the public and whoever does take office.

The Anti-War Candidate

Nader has staked out the strongest anti-war position on Iraq, calling for a unilateral but responsible withdrawal of U.S. troops, as well as military and civilian contractors, within six months, announcing a firm date for the U.S. presence to be replaced by a multinational peace-keeping force.

Nader would phase out the withdrawal in coordination with internationally supervised elections and continued rebuilding and humanitarian aid. Nader says this is something quite different from the installation of a puppet government and an ongoing corporate and military occupation.

Nader has said, "I wish [Kerry] would just repeat what he said when he was 27 years old before the Senate, which is, 'How do you tell a soldier to die for a mistake?'"

He says Kerry is trying to "out-Bush Bush" on Iraq, because Kerry has supported the idea of sending more troops to Iraq to control the violence. Although Kerry has expressed strong misgivings about the Bush administration's handling of the war, including the Abu Ghraib prison scandal, Kerry has said that we cannot afford to fail in Iraq, leaving the country as a source of instability in the Middle East.

Nader says, "The peace movement in this country is going to have a very interesting choice: whether they're going to basically support two pro-war candidates or whether they're going to support a muscular peace candidate." He has said that Kerry "is stuck in the Iraq quagmire the same way Bush is." In Kerry, "you see all the early phases of Lyndon Johnson in Vietnam."

Mike Keefe—www.cartoonstock.com

High Crimes and Misdemeanors

But Nader insists that his rhetoric is not aimed solely at Kerry, targeting Bush as a "messianic militarist" who led us into a quagmire with a "faulty and fabricated rationale for war."

More Nader on Bush: "When you plunge our country into war on a platform of fabrications and deceptions and you bring back thousands of American soldiers who are sick, injured, or dead, and that war is unconstitutionally authorized to begin with. Mr. Bush's behavior qualifies for the high crimes and misdemeanor impeachment clause of the Constitution."

Nader says that the Bush war in Iraq has weakened our national security by turning countries around the world against the U.S. and creating what he calls a terrorism "blowback" effect against us that will result from resentment of our invasion and occupation.

Reaching Out to the World

Beyond the Middle East, Nader's foreign policy is focused on humanitarian aid and limiting U.S. arms sales overseas. Nader's foreign policy priorities include

- ✓ Extending the resources of America to foreign countries through aid for public health measures, including drinking water safety, tobacco use control, and initiatives against flu epidemics and other infectious diseases such as AIDS, malaria, and tuberculosis. Work with the UN Development Program to provide aid and know-how in agriculture and health care. Also wants to improve international labor standards and support democratic institutions abroad.
- ✓ Cutting defense spending by $100 billion by reducing waste and fraud and eliminating redundant and unnecessary weapons, including the F-22 program, additional B-2 bombers, the Osprey, and other "gold-plated" weapons. He says defense cuts will help reduce the budget deficit.
- ✓ Supporting treaties that Bush has not, such as the small arms treaty, Comprehensive Test Ban Treaty, the verification protocol for the Biological Weapons Convention, and the Kyoto Protocol on global warming.
- ✓ Ending secret detentions and tribunals for citizens as part of war on terror. Against open borders—says we shouldn't criminalize our border, but we need to control it.

LAUGH TRACK

"John Kerry raised all of that money and bought himself an airplane, a campaign plane, for $10 million. Ralph Nader, not to be outdone, is having himself shipped across the country in a crate."

—David Letterman

The Economy

Nader's economic policy is driven by his battles against multi-national corporations. Nader is very much an anti-globalization candidate: He believes the U.S. should withdraw from NAFTA and GATT, stating that NAFTA and the World Trade Organization should be reworked to include environmental, social, and labor standards.

He says NAFTA and GATT are not free-trade agreements but corporate-managed trade. They're not win-win agreements because we're exporting jobs.

Nader's priorities for the economy include

- ✓ Opposing work visas for low-wage foreign workers who come to the U.S. and take high-tech and other jobs American workers have been trained for.
- ✓ Cutting off "corporate welfare" by increasing taxes on corporations and the wealthy.
- ✓ Reforming tax law by shifting taxation from workers' incomes and consumer essentials such as food and clothing to less productive behaviors such as alcohol consumption, smoking, gambling, and pollution.
- ✓ Fully funding education programs and preventive health care. He wants to stop the focus on standardized assessment in schools and shift to a civics-oriented program of instruction, teaching students how to be good public citizens in our democracy.
- ✓ Creating new jobs through investment in labor-intensive public works programs and improvements, rebuilding our roads and schools.
- ✓ Creating a clean energy policy that is renewable, sustainable, and environmentally friendly—investing in renewable energy such as wind and solar power as well as building more energy-efficient homes, cars, and businesses.
- ✓ Cracking down on corporate crime by funding prosecution of corporate and executive criminals, shifting power in corporate governance to shareholders, paying back ill-gotten gains, and reigning in executive pay. Nader says that corporations should not have all the same rights as humans, as has been held in the Supreme Court. Nader says this gives corporations the advantage in numerous legal issues.
- ✓ Ending poverty through progressive taxation, creating jobs, equal pay for women, affordable child care, living wages for all workers, and restoring the critical social safety net.
- ✓ Creating an "Employee Bill of Rights" that would include a living wage, access to health care, no unilateral reductions in benefits and pensions, protection of employee privacy, and repeal of the Taft-Hartley Act, which makes unionizing difficult.

★ ***WHAT HE SAYS:***
"This may be the only candidacy that is opposed overwhelmingly by those who agree on the issues." —Ralph Nader

★ ***WHAT HE WANTS YOU TO HEAR:***
I'm for all the liberal positions the Democrats say they're for, and I won't drift toward the center to get votes.

★ ***BUT DON'T FORGET:***
I have virtually no chance of getting elected, and I may keep Kerry from getting elected too.

The Environment

Nader has been a prominent protector of the environment since the earliest days of his consumer advocacy. Nader has founded groups such as the Clean Water Action Project and the Resource Consumption Alliance. He was instrumental in passing the Safe Drinking Water Act, and many of his books concern environmental issues such as air pollution, clean water, preserving our forests and federal lands, and the dangers of atomic energy.

Beginning in the 1970s, Nader spearheaded many of the environmental protection initiatives that are at the root of the Green movement, including establishment of the Environmental Protection Agency (EPA), to the benefit of the public. Nader ran for president in 1996 and 2000 on the Green Party ticket.

Nader's priorities for the environment include

- ✓ Making environmental protection a priority for all government policies, including energy, trade, agriculture, transportation, development, and land use.
- ✓ Raising standards for toxicity levels in our air and water.
- ✓ Charging agribusiness for water use.
- ✓ Eliminating highway projects that lead to urban sprawl, air pollution, and global warming.

- ✓ Controlling bio-engineered products such as beef and produce that can have unintended and dangerous consequences (although this is debatable and as yet scientifically unproven).
- ✓ Ending all commercial logging in National Forests and providing more funds for National Parks.

Social Issues

Nader has been on the front line of protecting citizens' legal rights, especially as they relate to corporations and free access to government information. He was instrumental in getting the Freedom of Information Act passed in 1974, a law that provides for open citizen access to government records and documents.

Nader leans way to the left on social issues. His priorities include

- ✓ Supporting the full platform of NOW, the National Organization of Women, which has an 11-point feminist agenda that includes "feminization of power," equality of pay for women, passing the Equal Rights Amendment, access to safe and legal abortions as well as family planning, access to quality child care, and fighting for homemakers' rights that regard marriage as an equal economic partnership, and fighting for the rights of older women by ending inequality in Social Security, pension, and health care plans.
- ✓ Supporting abortion specifically. Nader says it's not the government's role to tell a woman to have a child.
- ✓ Supporting affirmative action as well as gay marriage. Nader supports full equal rights for gay men and women, including allowing them to serve openly in the military. He opposes Bush's proposed constitutional amendment against gay marriage, saying it would be the only time we have amended the constitution to restrict the rights and freedoms of a class of people. He supports strengthening hate crime legislation.
- ✓ Supporting passage of the End Racial Profiling Act, which would dissuade law enforcement from profiling by gathering race data on suspects—says this is specifically a problem for Muslims and

Arab Americans. He also opposes extending the Patriot Act and urges examination of post-9/11 investigative procedures put into place by the Bush administration.

Gun Control, Crime, and the Death Penalty

As the anti-war candidate, ending the "war on drugs" is the cornerstone of Nader's law enforcement policy. Nader believes drug abuse is a public health problem, not a crime. He argues that the war on drugs has been costly and unsuccessful, and says we need to turn our efforts toward social programs that will eliminate the cause of abuse as well as support and recovery programs for addicts.

Nader says that bringing some illegal drugs within the law by taxing, regulating, and controlling them will reduce street crime and violence.

Nader supported the Brady gun control bill, trigger locks, gun licensing, as well as banning assault weapons. He strongly opposes the death penalty, saying it does not deter and is discriminatory. He wants a moratorium on all executions.

LAUGH TRACK

"John Kerry told the press he is not asking Ralph Nader to drop out of the race, and today President Bush said, 'Hey, me neither.'"

—Jay Leno

Health Care and Education

Nader says we need to get the insurance companies out of administering health care, increase patient choice, expand coverage, and save money. He says we spend more money per capita on health care than any industrialized nation, yet 45 million Americans have no coverage. He wants a single-payer program with full medical coverage for all Americans throughout their lives, although his plan does not talk about how to fund it.

Nader wants to shift the emphasis in education away from high-stakes standardized testing; he says it makes the curriculum focus too narrow and has a negative impact on student learning. He wants schools to infuse their curriculums with civic experiences that connect classroom learning to the outside world and how to participate in democracy by getting involved in elections and civic debate.

Electoral Reform

Nader pushes for electoral reform as one of the top issues in his campaign. He says participation in democracy has been dampened by corporate control of campaign finance. He wants to publicly fund all elections, end gerrymandering of districts that make most races one-party affairs, and get rid of obstacles to third-party and independent candidates such as himself.

He says the two-party system is controlled by corporate interests, and a change in voting systems to instant run-off voting would help bring back the vigor to our democracy.

Nader also wants to lower the minimum voting age to sixteen as part of his plan to teach school-age kids about the importance of voting and civic participation. He says most kids that age work and pay taxes, and should have the right to vote because they are often treated as adults in criminal trials.

Parker—www.cartoonstock.com

WHO ARE THESE GUYS?

You may not be aware of it, but Ralph Nader is not the only independent, third-party, or write-in candidate in this year's presidential election. As usual, there's a long list of candidates for voters to choose from—everything from a New Age "Wholistic Physician, Human Ecologist, and Artist" to a self-proclaimed fascist who predicts that "the United States will be reduced from its present size to a small triangular-shaped land mass through the loss of many coastal states."

At last count, nearly three dozen presidential hopefuls have stated their intentions to run for the highest office in the land (see Table 10.1 for a list of major third-party candidates). Their campaigns have varying degrees of seriousness, funding, and hope—but all of their campaign Web sites make for some interesting reading. Some highlights:

- A.J. "Victor" Albritton (Alabama)—Nominee of the "American Republican Party." His objective is to be "the American candidate who is also the Victorian candidate. The Victorian Era to be the New Model Victorian Era—from the male point of view." Whatever that means. He probably doesn't support the Equal Rights Amendment.
- Larry D. Hines (Texas)—Sought the Libertarian Party nomination in 2000 as "The Openly Gay Candidate for U.S. President," and then tried to run as the candidate for Jesse Ventura's Independence Party before that party crashed and burned. Back again for another try as an Independent in 2004.
- Georgia Hough (Georgia)—High school teacher with a master's degree in history, she says that teaching social studies has given her "a good understanding of the underlying issues driving our government and our economy."
- Lawrence Ray Topham (Utah)—Has run for various state and local offices in Utah and has declared himself "Secretary of State of the State of Utah and Acting Governor during martial law." Topham is a man of action: He declared martial law in Utah in 1997 of his own initiative because everyone is using "fake money" not backed by gold or silver. On his Web site, he lists his favorite food as "wheat."

- ✓ Keith R. Judd (Massachusetts)—Describing himself as a "bongo drums musician," he has run for mayor of Albuquerque and governor of New Mexico. Ran for president in 2000, but there are as yet no overt signs of his run for the White House in 2004.

Table 10.1 Third-Party Candidates

Party	Presidential Candidate	VP Candidate
American	Diane Templin	Al Moore
Constitution	Michael Peroutka	Chuck Baldwin
Green	Several still running	Several still running
Libertarian	Michael Badnarik	Richard Campagna
Reform	Ralph Nader	Jan Pierce
Socialist USA	Walt Brown	Mary Alice Herbert

Platform	Web Site
Isolationist, anti free trade	**www.theamericanparty.org**
Christian, government rooted in Biblical law	**www.constitution-party.net**
Environmentalist, progressive on social issues	**www.gp.org**
Individual liberty, free-market/free-trade economy, non-interventionist foreign policy	**www.lp.org**
Government and economic reform	**www.reformparty.org**
Socialism, anti-war	**www.sp-usa.org**

"Politics is the art of the possible."
—Otto von Bismarck

Candidate Comparison Guide

The following chapter summarizes the positions of Bush, Kerry, and Nader on the top issues in the 2004 campaign. This chapter provides a brief recap of where the candidates stand on these issues so you can compare their positions side by side.

You can also write in which position you prefer in the far right column of the chart to help you see how the candidates match up with what you believe. After you have compared the candidates on the issues, turn to Chapter 12, "Candidate Match Survey," to help you finalize your decision on the candidate that will best represent you in the White House.

These summaries of policy are compiled from the candidates' public statements, speeches, ads, and campaign websites. Keep in mind that we do not support any one candidate's position on a particular issue over any other candidate's position, nor can we vouch for or predict the candidate's ability to carry out the policy or platform position once in office.

Remember that the president cannot enact laws, only support or advocate a particular policy agenda, and many of these platform positions are crafted and influenced by the candidates' political parties.

Foreign Policy

War in Iraq

George W. Bush	John Kerry
Actively pursued U.S.-led coalition invasion of Iraq as part of the "War on Terror." Initially said the war was to stop Iraqi WMDs, and then changed objective to include toppling Saddam Hussein and bringing democracy to Iraq. Invaded without support from the U.N. or other allies by building a "coalition of the willing."	Voted for resolution authorizing use of force in Iraq as a means of putting muscle behind diplomatic efforts to halt Iraqi WMDs. Later voted against a measure funding further military activity in Iraq to voice displeasure over Bush's invasion without U.N. approval or diplomatic efforts. Says Bush misled on pre-war intelligence about WMDs.

Iraq Withdrawal

George W. Bush	John Kerry
Opposed U.N. involvement in post-war Iraq, but now has sought U.N. support of peacekeeping and re-building efforts. Installed U.N.-supported Iraqi interim government and calls for elections by January 31. Plans for troops to stay in Iraq through 2006.	Says the exit strategy is victory—we need to be successful. Says Bush didn't plan for re-building the country or winning the peace. Wants to spread responsibility for humanitarian aid, government support, and peacekeeping to U.N. and other countries to spread the burden. "Get troops home as fast as possible with honor and the job accomplished the way it needs to be."

Ralph Nader	Who Do You Agree With?
Opposed invasion and occupation of Iraq and says Bush should be impeached for plunging the U.S. into an un-authorized war based on "fabrications and deceptions." Calls Bush a "messianic militarist" for leading us into a "quagmire."	

Ralph Nader	Who Do You Agree With?
Says Bush invasion of Iraq has increased the chances of a terror attack by creating a breeding ground for terrorists. Advocates complete withdrawal of U.S. troops and civilian contractors from Iraq by the end of 2004, replacing them with a multinational peacekeeping force.	

Abu Ghraib

George W. Bush	John Kerry
Maintains that Iraqi prison abuse by U.S. soldiers was the product of an isolated few "bad apples." Apologized to Arabs and Americans. Says the abuse was not systemic and the abusers will be tried and punished. Supports Defense Secretary Donald Rumsfeld in the face of criticism from those who call for him to resign. Wants to demolish the Abu Ghraib prison with consent of Iraqi government.	Calls for Defense Secretary Rumsfeld to resign. Says that if he is elected as president, he "will demand accountability from those who serve, and [he] will take responsibility for their actions. Says "the chain of command goes all the way to the Oval Office."

Middle East

George W. Bush	John Kerry
Calls for a "forward strategy of freedom" to ensure peace and democracy in the Middle East. This strategy includes creating a Palestinian state and demanding democratic reforms in the governance of the Palestinian Authority. Bush says Israel must freeze settlement construction, dismantle unauthorized outposts, and not set up walls or fences that would prejudice final negotiations.	Wants to maintain a steady policy of support for Israel, calling it our most important ally. Says Bush ignored the Palestinian conflict far too long, increasing the terror threat. Says Bush road map for peace is on the right track, but came too late and has not been fully supported by the administration. Calls for a Palestinian state and full engagement in the peace process from the U.S. and would appoint a presidential envoy to move the process forward.

Ralph Nader	Who Do You Agree With?
Calls for an independent, international commission to investigate abuse, as called for by the Geneva Protocol, and payment of restitution by the U.S. to all prisoners whose rights were violated. Asks Bush to renounce inhumane interrogation techniques and ban the use of corporate contractors in interrogation and prison administration.	

Ralph Nader	Who Do You Agree With?
Favors creation of a Palestinian state and denounces unconditional U.S. support of Israel. Sympathetic to the hardship Palestinians face; he wants an open, balanced dialogue with the twin goals of Israeli security and a Palestinian state.	

Afghanistan

George W. Bush	John Kerry
Calls for more than $1 billion for reconstruction efforts, including building roads, using NATO forces for security, and a new constitution guaranteeing free elections.	Says we need to increase U.N. efforts to secure the peace and maintain focus here in destroying the Al Quaeda network and Osama Bin Laden. Says U.S. has won the war but hasn't secured the peace, as in Iraq. Says we must "drain the swamps of terrorists."

Pre-Emption Policy

George W. Bush	John Kerry
Established pre-emptive strikes against states supporting terrorism as a formal and major shift in U.S. foreign policy. Pre-emption is the basis for Bush foreign policy, and he states it is necessary to prevent terror attacks on the U.S.	Says Bush's policy of pre-emptive and unilateral war is the most reckless foreign policy in modern history and threatens America's safety and prosperity. Says the policy has squandered goodwill of the world, alienated our allies, overextended our troops, and compromised our security.

Ralph Nader	Who Do You Agree With?
Says the war in Afghanistan is a quagmire, just like Iraq. Says torture, degradation, and inhumane treatment have been the Bush administration mode of operation in Iraq, Afghanistan, and Guantanamo Bay. Says Bush "burned down a haystack to try to find a couple of needles" in Afghanistan. Nader would have organized an international force to search for and arrest Bin Laden.	

Ralph Nader	Who Do You Agree With?
Says unilateral, pre-emptive attacks violate international law and would focus on humanitarian aid overseas.	

Increase U.S. Troops

George W. Bush	John Kerry
Has increased number of U.S. troops in Iraq and widened the Army's "stop-loss" program, which prevents thousands of soldiers in Afghanistan and Iraq from retiring or otherwise leaving the military prior to completing their deployment in combat zones. Has not called for an increase in the total number of U.S. troops in the military.	Says NATO and U.N. involvement in Iraq peacekeeping will free up 20,000 U.S. troops. Says Bush has stretched Army too thin, so he would temporarily increase the size of the active-duty Army by 40,000 troops to help meet new challenges we face.

Parker—caglecartoons.com

Ralph Nader	Who Do You Agree With?
Is against overseas troop deployments and says we need to withdraw U.S. troops from Iraq by the end of 2004. Says having troops in Iraq imperils U.S. security, drains our economy by shifting focus from domestic issues, and prevents Iraqi self-rule.	

Defense Budgets

George W. Bush	John Kerry
His budget increases defense spending by $15.3 billion. Wants pay increases for military personnel to build on recent increases of 4% or more. Wants to transform military by developing "next-generation" weapons such as unmanned air and water vehicles, stealth ships, and subs equipped with long-range cruise missiles.	Calls for a Military Family Bill of Rights to provide competitive pay, good housing, decent health care, and quality education for soldiers and their families. Also calls for state-of-the art equipment and training. Says he will never reduce special compensation for soldiers such as family separation and hazardous duty pay, unlike Bush, and he would provide assistance to families if a service member is killed. Says a modern military means smarter, more versatile equipment, better intelligence, advanced communications, long-range airpower, and highly mobile ground troops.

Missile Defense

George W. Bush	John Kerry
Withdrew from the Anti-Ballistic Missile treaty with Russia, and provides $9 billion in the 2004 budget to begin deployment of defenses against long-range ballistic missiles, including new interceptors to be deployed over the next two years. Says his missile defense policy is a "search for security, not a search for advantage."	Voted against Reagan's "Star-Wars" missile defense system in the 1980s. Says U.S. is more likely to be attacked by a weapon of mass destruction that has been smuggled into the country aboard a ship than delivered on a ballistic missile. Supports nonproliferation and arms control treaties.

Ralph Nader	Who Do You Agree With?
Wants to cut defense spending by $100 billion by reducing waste and fraud and eliminating redundant and unnecessary weapons, including the F-22 program, additional B-2 bombers, the Osprey, and other "gold-plated" weapons. He says defense cuts will help reduce the budget deficit.	

Ralph Nader	Who Do You Agree With?
Wants to cut defense spending overall and opposes a national missile defense system.	

Economy and Government

Jobs

George W. Bush	John Kerry
Focuses on creating new jobs by stimulating the economy through tax cuts for individuals and businesses. His Jobs and Growth Tax Relief Reconciliation Act of 2003 creates investment opportunity for businesses by providing dividend and capital gains tax relief. The new tax law also increases limits in expensing equipment for small businesses from $25,000 to $100,000.	Plans to replace jobs lost during Bush administration and create a total of 10 million jobs in his administration by establishing a new manufacturing jobs credit, investing in new and alternative energy industries, restoring technology, and stopping layoffs in education.

Tax Cuts

George W. Bush	John Kerry
Tax cuts are the primary focus of his economic plan. Wants to make some parts of his tax cuts permanent so that they don't expire after 2005. These include the increase in the child tax credit, elimination of the estate tax, and the new tax incentives for small business investment.	Wants to reform America's international tax system to end tax breaks that encourage companies to move jobs overseas by eliminating the ability of companies to defer paying taxes on foreign income. Wants to close international tax loopholes and use the funds from changing international taxes to cut the corporate tax rate by 5%. Says this tax plan will stimulate the economy by bringing jobs and industry back to the U.S. Will keep "middle class" tax cuts such as child tax credit and elimination of marriage penalty.

Ralph Nader	Who Do You Agree With?
Plans to create new jobs through investment in labor-intensive public works programs and improvements, rebuilding our roads and schools, and requiring equitable trade with foreign countries. Opposes H1-B and L1 work visas for low-wage foreign workers who come to the U.S. and take high-tech and other jobs American workers have been trained for.	

Ralph Nader	Who Do You Agree With?
Wants to cut off "corporate welfare" by increasing taxes on corporations and the wealthy. Would reform tax law by shifting taxation from workers' incomes and consumer essentials such as food and clothing to our least productive behaviors such as alcohol consumption, smoking, gambling, and pollution.	

Budget Deficits

George W. Bush	John Kerry
Says half the budget deficit was caused by recession, one quarter of it caused by war in Iraq, and one quarter of it caused by the Bush tax cuts. But he says the tax cuts will put money back into the budget by stimulating the economy. Says the best way to cut the deficit is keep the tax cuts in place and hold the line on spending. Says his plan will cut the deficit in half within five years.	Says Bush tax cuts for wealthiest Americans are forcing the government to spend $1 billion per day more than it takes in. Wants a smaller, smarter government and will repeal all Bush tax cuts for Americans who make more than $200,000 per year. Will implement the McCain-Kerry commission plan on corporate welfare to eliminate special interest group loopholes and spending projects. Says government grew under Bush, but he will cut its size by reducing energy costs, making it more efficient, and reducing fraud and abuse.

Ralph Nader	Who Do You Agree With?
Criticizes Bush tax cuts as expanding the divide between luxuries of the rich and necessities of the poor and middle class. Says deficit is caused by tax cuts, corporate welfare, and redundant spending on the "military industrial complex." Wants to shift spending from defense to critical programs such as infrastructure, transit, public works, schools, clinics, libraries, forests, parks, sustainable energy, and pollution controls. Would cut $100 billion from the military budget to reduce the deficit.	

Social Security

George W. Bush	John Kerry
Bush's plan to strengthen Social Security includes support for Individual Development Accounts—tax-free savings matches for low-income Americans, tax relief, voluntary investment of Social Security taxes in personal retirement accounts, and minimizing risk for workers by allowing them to sell company stock and diversify into other investment options. Bush's plan also calls for allowing "catch-up" retirement plan contributions for women who took time off work to raise children, as well as creating property rights in personal retirement accounts for divorced women and expanded benefits for widows.	Says Bush tax cuts and deficits will require cuts to Social Security. Says the way to keep Social Security fiscally sound is to roll back tax cuts for Americans who make more than $200,000 and to reform the estate tax.

Ralph Nader	Who Do You Agree With?
Says Social Security is "solid until 2042 without any changes or benefit cuts." Focuses on restoring retirement security through reforms of corporate retirement plan and investor abuses, including unfairly changing retirement plan rules, ending pension plans by selling corporate divisions, and cutting employees out of pension plans by reclassifying them as contract workers.	

Free Trade

George W. Bush	John Kerry
Supported admitting China into the World Trade Organization (WTO) and Permanent Normal Trade Relations (PNTR) with China. Supports expanding NAFTA to include all the Western Hemisphere, but imposed tariffs on foreign steel that violated WTO rules. Lifted the steel tariffs after threats of retaliation from U.S. trading partners.	Plans to order a 120-day review of all trade agreements to ensure that trading partners adhere to their labor and environment obligations and make sure the agreements are enforceable and balanced for American workers. Supports NAFTA and PNTR for China.

Agriculture

George W. Bush	John Kerry
Supports farm savings accounts, trade agreements that end export subsidies, and promoting conservation on working lands. Supports ethanol as a renewable fuel we can create domestically, and says getting rid of estate taxes helps farmers pass on their lands to new generations.	Supports increased funding for agricultural conservation programs, rural community development programs, and nutrition market development programs. Says renewable energy such as ethanol, biomass, wind, and biodiesel produced on farms will reduce foreign energy dependence and pollution. Supports a ban on packer ownership of livestock, which drives small farmers out of business.

Ralph Nader	Who Do You Agree With?
Replace NAFTA and WTO with fair trade agreements that pull up labor, environmental, and consumer standards. Exchange corporate-managed, profit-driven trade for fair trade.	

Ralph Nader	Who Do You Agree With?
Says we must challenge growing concentration of wealth by agriculture, chemical, biotech, and financial corporations, which gives them control over farming and causes misallocation of resources. Wants to shift government policy to ensure open and competitive markets, promote sustainable farming practices, and prevent pollution of natural resources.	

Energy and Environment

George W. Bush	John Kerry
Proposes spending $1.2 billion on developing hydrogen fuel to stop dependence on foreign oil. Goal is to produce hydrogen fuel cell vehicles for use by 2020. Clear Skies initiative proposes reducing power plant emissions by 70%, saving consumers $1 billion annually in compliance costs. His Healthy Forests initiative is a plan to restore forests to natural, fire-resistant conditions through clearing. Budget includes $4.4 billion for climate change research and $500 million in tax incentives to improve energy efficiency and promote renewable energy.	Says we should invent our way out of foreign oil dependency instead of drilling our way out. This means developing alternative energy sources such as hydrogen and improving energy efficiency in homes, schools, and businesses and developing renewable sources of electricity. Proposes a "Conservation Covenant" requiring energy and mineral royalties from public lands to be reinvested into protecting the land. Promotes "Clean and Green Communities" by coordinating efforts to reduce urban sprawl and traffic congestion.

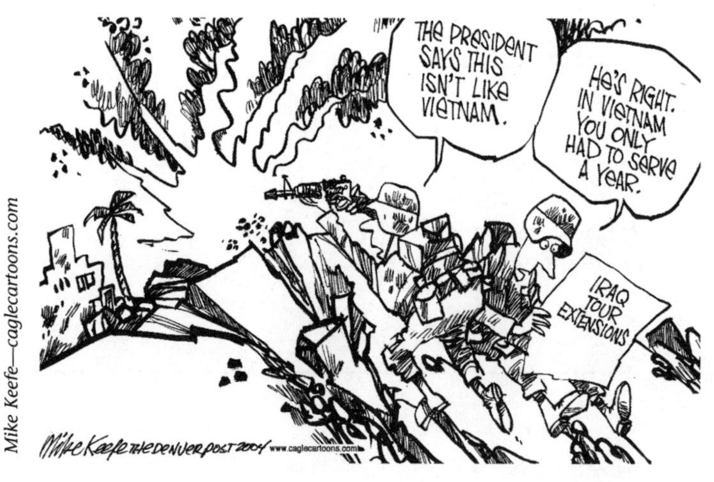

Mike Keefe—caglecartoons.com

Ralph Nader	Who Do You Agree With?
Wants to make environmental protection a priority for all government policies, including energy, trade, agriculture, transportation, development and land use. Says we should raise standards for toxicity levels in our air and water and charge agribusiness for water use. Eliminate highway projects that lead to urban sprawl, air pollution, and global warming, control bioengineered products that can have unintended and dangerous consequences, and stop all commercial logging in National Forests.	

Campaign Finance

George W. Bush	John Kerry
Signed the Bipartisan Campaign Reform Act of 2002, preventing corporations and unions from making "soft money" contributions to campaigns and raising individual contributor limits. The law also created new disclosure requirements for campaign donors.	Voted YES on the Bipartisan Campaign Reform Act of 2002. Has accepted less than 1% of his presidential campaign funding from PACs. Has spent more than $6 million of his own money on the campaign.

Civil Rights

Abortion

George W. Bush	John Kerry
Opposes abortion except in cases of life-threatening risk, incest, and rape. Signed the Partial-Birth Abortion Act of 2003. Accepts FDA approval of the RU-486 "abortion pill" but is concerned that it will promote more abortions. Blocked funds to international groups that offer abortion counseling. Says taxpayer funds shouldn't be used to pay for abortions or abortion counseling.	Believes Constitution protects women's right to choose and says he will only support pro-choice judges for the Supreme Court. Supports family planning and says health plans should assure women of contraceptive coverage. Does not support partial-birth abortion ban.

Ralph Nader	Who Do You Agree With?
Favors publicly financed elections and electoral reform to make elections more open to candidates beyond the two major parties. Such reforms include proportional representation, instant run-off voting, and including third-party and independent candidates in televised debates.	

Ralph Nader	Who Do You Agree With?
Supports the National Organization for Women position that abortion is a matter of life and death for women—not a choice. Supports the NOW agenda of access to safe and legal abortions, birth control, and reproductive education. Opposes any attempts to restrict these rights by law or Constitutional amendment.	

Affirmative Action

George W. Bush	John Kerry
Opposes quotas and affirmative action. Says quotas don't work and they "pit people against each other." Supports "affirmative access," guaranteeing admittance to a university if you're in the top 10% of a high school graduating class. Enhance access to the middle class by "challenging the soft bigotry of low expectations."	Wants to "mend, not end" affirmative action, by shifting emphasis from group preferences to economic empowerment for all disadvantaged citizens. Signed the "New Agenda for a New Decade" manifesto, which says "we should resist an 'identity politics' that confers rights and entitlements on groups and instead affirm our common rights and responsibilities as citizens."

Gay Rights

George W. Bush	John Kerry
Calls for a Constitutional amendment defining marriage as between a man and a woman. Wants a "morally traditional and socially inclusive" policy. Says states should be able to define their own alternative legal arrangements other than marriage within the Constitutional amendment.	Opposed the Defense of Marriage Act (DOMA) and supports rights for gay couples such as access to pensions, health insurance, family leave, and other basic legal protections. Supports same-sex civil unions but has said that marriage should be between a man and a woman. Opposes a constitutional amendment banning gay marriage. Does not support the law allowing gay marriage in his home state of Massachusetts, but believes marriage law should be left to individual states.

Ralph Nader	Who Do You Agree With?
Supports affirmative action policies and says progress so far on the road to equality for African-Americans has been too slow, especially in the economic arena.	

Ralph Nader	Who Do You Agree With?
Supports full equal rights for gay men and women, including allowing them to serve openly in the military. Opposes Bush's proposed constitutional amendment against gay marriage, saying it would be the only time we have amended the constitution to restrict the rights and freedoms of a class of people. Supports strengthening hate crime legislation.	

Homeland Security

Patriot Act

George W. Bush	John Kerry
Need to renew key aspects of the Patriot Act set to expire in 2005. Must continue to give law enforcement personnel every tool they need to protect us, including the Patriot Act, which allows federal law enforcement to better share information, track terrorists, disrupt their cells, and seize their assets. Don't let the Patriot Act expire because the terrorists threat will not expire. Created Office of Homeland Security and numerous other government initiatives designed to protect nation from terror attacks. Supports the policy of labeling U.S. citizens "enemy combatants" if they are involved in terrorist activities.	Keep Patriot Act provisions that help war on terror, such as increasing penalties for terrorism and adding new federal terror crimes, but also need to improve Patriot Act by enhancing efforts to stop money laundering and improving information sharing between intelligence agencies and law enforcement. Need to stop abuses of Patriot Act such as allowing FBI to attend any meeting, "sneak and peek" searches, unwarranted seizures of library and business records. Against labeling U.S. citizens "enemy combatants."

Wright—caglecartoons.com

Ralph Nader	Who Do You Agree With?
Supports repeal of the Patriot Act. Says Muslims and Arab-Americans bear the brunt of dragnet, arbitrary practices. Says civil liberties and due process of law are being eroded by practices such as secret detentions, arrests without charges, no access to attorneys, and use of "secret" evidence.	

Immigration

George W. Bush	John Kerry
Wants to increase budget to better enforce existing immigration laws. Launched initiatives to protect our borders, including tracking procedures for foreign students, unmanned aerial vehicle patrols, improved airport security, creation of the Terrorist Screening Center (which consolidates terrorist watchlists), and capturing more complete arrival and departure data for those requiring visas, including photo and biometric information.	Criticizes holding foreign detainees for indefinite periods for questioning without cause. Says there should be no new laws preventing release of information about detainee abuse. Wants to stop using anti-terror laws as an assault on immigration. Says Attorney General John Ashcroft has weakened the immigration review and appeal process by arbitrarily arresting and detaining immigrants guilty of only routine visa violations.

Social Issues

Death Penalty

George W. Bush	John Kerry
Supports the death penalty because he believes it deters crime. Does not believe in use of death penalty for revenge. Says DNA evidence should be used to confirm guilt before execution. Says death penalty clemency should be for unfair legal process or proof of innocence, not for repentant criminals.	Against the death penalty except in cases of international and domestic terrorism. Supports a moratorium on federal executions until DNA testing can be used to ensure that all those on death row are guilty.

Ralph Nader	Who Do You Agree With?
Wants to end secret detentions and arrests without charges. Says there should be no military tribunals for civilians. Says these acts represent a "perilous diminishment of judicial authority in favor of concentrated power in the executive branch."	

Ralph Nader	Who Do You Agree With?
Strongly opposes the death penalty. Says it does not deter and is discriminatory. Wants a moratorium on all executions.	

Drug Abuse

George W. Bush	John Kerry
Announced 3-year, $600 million federal program designed to help addicts have access to effective treatment, including faith-based and community-based programs. Says program will provide treatment to 300,000 more Americans who need help.	Believes focus should be on keeping illegal drugs out of our country and our communities as well as reducing demand for illegal drugs. Supports aggressively targeting traffickers and dealers, as well as sufficiently funding drug prevention and treatment programs.

Gun Control

George W. Bush	John Kerry
Says we should enforce existing laws more aggressively, including the ban on automatic weapons. Supports instant background checks (as opposed to 3-day waiting periods) at gun shows and gun shops. Says we need to keep guns out of the hands of the wrong people. Supports voluntary trigger locks—not mandatory—and says government should fund a program to distribute trigger locks to the public. Supports raising the minimum age for juveniles to carry guns. Wants to restrict lawsuits against gun makers.	Says all Americans should have the right to own guns, but rights come with responsibilities. Says we should vigorously enforce existing laws by cracking down on gun runners, corrupt dealers, and straw buyers, who circumvent the laws. Wants to close the gun show loophole, which allows people to buy guns without background checks, and require all handguns to be sold with safety locks. Says we need to repair the background check system.

Ralph Nader	Who Do You Agree With?
Believes drug abuse is a public health problem, not a crime. Says the war on drugs has been costly and unsuccessful, and says we need to turn our efforts toward support recovery programs for addicts as well as social programs that will eliminate the cause of abuse. Says bringing some illegal drugs within the law by taxing, regulating, and controlling them will reduce street crime and violence.	

Ralph Nader	Who Do You Agree With?
Supports the Brady gun control bill, trigger locks, as well as banning assault weapons. Says we should look at weapons the same way we look at cars: All owners and operators should get a license.	

Education

George W. Bush	John Kerry
Passed the No Child Left Behind (NCLB) education reform act with bipartisan support in Congress. Says NCLB helps children by supporting early learning, measuring student performance, providing information for parents on underperforming schools, giving families options when schools are underperforming, and ensuring that schools have more resources. Says this comprehensive program is a historic reform of our nation's failing schools.	Supported NCLB but says Bush has not properly funded it. Proposes a New National Education Trust Fund to guarantee federal funds for federally mandated programs such as NCLB. Wants to change NCLB to focus on ensuring that all students are prepared for college and schools are not just test prep institutions. Says priorities should be higher teacher pay, higher standards, and ensuring classroom discipline.

Poverty

George W. Bush	John Kerry
His "compassionate conservatism" agenda calls for faith-based and community-based initiatives to help solve problems faced by the poor, the homeless, at-risk youth, addicts, elders in need, and families moving from welfare to work. Says government should work together with faith-based programs to help those in need. Says faith-based programs should receive government funds. Created USA Freedom Corps to encourage volunteering.	Supports government partnering with non-profit and for-profit organizations to provide services such as child care and after-school programs. Supported the welfare reform laws, including replacement of federal welfare guarantee with state block grants. Says we need to finish welfare reform by moving all able workers into jobs and cutting poverty rate in half. Reinforce values of work and responsibility, and guarantee that no family with a full-time worker should live in poverty.

Ralph Nader	Who Do You Agree With?
Says education is primarily the responsibility of state and local governments. States that federal government should keep what he calls undermining influences out of schools, including commercialism and school vouchers. Wants to shift emphasis away from high-stakes standardized testing—says it makes curriculum focus too narrow and has negative impact on learning. Wants schools to infuse curriculums with civic experiences.	

Ralph Nader	Who Do You Agree With?
Says we should attack corporate welfare recipients instead of poor recipients of public aid who need it most. Says we can end poverty through truly progressive taxation, ending corporate subsidies and military budget waste, creating jobs, equal pay for women, funding child care programs, providing a living wage for all workers, and restoring the social safety net.	

Health Care

George W. Bush	John Kerry
Wants to commit up to $400 billion to modernize Medicare over the next 10 years. Plan would give all Medicare beneficiaries access to prescription drug coverage without government dictating drug choice, choice of individual health care plan like that government employees enjoy, choice of doctor and treatment location, and full coverage for disease prevention such as screenings for cancer, diabetes, and osteoporosis. Wants to implement medical liability reform to reduce health care costs. Supports passing a Patients' Bill of Rights that says doctors should decide treatment, not insurance companies.	Says he will cap catastrophic medical costs for all Americans at $50,000 and reduce premiums for everyone by $1,000 through tax reform. Says he will give every American access to the same plan members of Congress have (the Federal Employees Health Care Benefits Program). Wants to ensure that health care is guaranteed through Medicaid for every child who is within 300% of poverty-level income. Supported bill to allow import of prescription drugs from Canada and voted yes on including prescription drugs in Medicare.

For more information about the candidates' positions on the issues, go to the candidates' official campaign web sites:

www.georgewbush.com

www.johnkerry.com

www.votenader.com

Ralph Nader	Who Do You Agree With?
Says we need to get insurance companies out of administering health care, increase patient choice, expand coverage, and save money. Wants a single-payer program with full medical coverage for all Americans throughout their lives.	

"Those who stand for nothing fall for anything."
—Alexander Hamilton

12

Candidate Match Survey

Respond to the statements in this Candidate Match Survey and you'll see how your views match up with the candidates' positions on the issues.

This survey is a representative sample of the candidates' positions on key issues in this election. You can also compare their platforms side by side, using the Comparison Guide in Chapter 11, starting on page 157, and go to the candidates' Web sites to learn more about their platforms:

www.georgewbush.com

www.johnkerry.com

www.votenader.com

It's Quick and Easy

Respond to each of the following statements by writing the following in the answer blank next to the statements:

Strongly Agree, Agree, Disagree, or Strongly Disagree (you can use the initials SA, A, D, SD)

When you have finished, you will receive instructions about how to tally your score.

1. The war in Iraq is a quagmire. ______
2. The U.S. should hand over peacekeeping duties in Iraq to the U.N. ______
3. The war in Iraq is a vital part of the War on Terror. ______
4. We should withdraw our troops from Iraq immediately. ______
5. We should add more troops in Iraq to make sure we get the job done. ______
6. War in Iraq increases likelihood of a terror attack. ______
7. Prison abuse in Abu Ghraib was not systemic. ______
8. A foreign policy of pre-emptive strikes is reckless and threatens U.S. safety. ______
9. Ballistic missile defense is critical to our security. ______
10. Tax cuts help the economy and create more jobs. ______
11. Investing in alternative energy sources will create more jobs. ______
12. We should shift taxation from income, food, and clothing to alcohol, smoking, gambling, and pollution. ______
13. The best way to cut the deficit is to keep tax cuts in place and hold the line on spending. ______
14. Social Security is in good financial shape until 2042. ______
15. We should replace NAFTA and the WTO with trade agreements that increase labor, environmental, and consumer standards. ______
16. We should invent our way out of dependence on foreign oil, not drill our way out. ______

17. We should not drill for oil in the Alaska National Wildlife Refuge. ______
18. Elections should be publicly financed—no corporate, PAC, or individual donations. ______
19. Partial-birth abortions should be banned. ______
20. Abortion should be outlawed except in cases of rape, incest, or life-threatening risk. ______
21. Affirmative action works, but it needs to be fixed. ______
22. There should be a constitutional amendment banning gay marriage. ______
23. Same-sex civil unions are an appropriate legal protection for the rights of gay couples. ______
24. The Patriot Act is critical to defending our nation against terror attacks. ______
25. Detaining foreign non-combatants for questioning is necessary for homeland security. ______
26. The death penalty should never be used as a punishment. ______
27. Keeping illegal drugs out of our country and curbing demand is the best way to stop the drug problem. ______
28. A safety course and a license should be required for all gun owners before purchase. ______
29. Liability lawsuits against gun makers should be restricted. ______
30. No Child Left Behind is the best way to guarantee good schools for all students. ______
31. Government-funded faith-based programs are a critical part of providing aid to the needy. ______
32. Medicaid should be expanded to cover all children and more uninsured Americans. ______

How Do You Match Up?

Use the following answer key to tally your score. For each statement, circle the candidate that matches your response. For example, if you Strongly Agreed with statement 1, you would circle Nader. If you Disagreed with statement 1, you would circle Bush. If you had No Opinion, do not score the question.

Next, add up the number of responses you matched for each candidate to see how well their positions match your opinions on the issues. Write the totals for each candidate in the boxes at the end of the answer key.

	Strongly Agree	**Agree**	**Disagree**	**Strongly Disagree**
1.	Nader	Kerry	Bush	Bush
2.	Nader	Nader/Kerry	Bush	Bush
3.	Bush	Bush	Kerry	Nader
4.	Nader	Nader	Kerry	Bush
5.	Kerry	Kerry	Bush	Nader
6.	Nader	Kerry	Bush	Bush
7.	Bush	Bush	Kerry	Nader
8.	Nader/Kerry	Nader/Kerry	Bush	Bush
9.	Bush	Bush	Kerry/Nader	Kerry/Nader
10.	Bush	Bush	Kerry	Nader
11.	Kerry	Kerry		
12.	Nader	Nader	Kerry	Bush
13.	Bush	Bush	Kerry	Nader
14.	Nader	Nader	Bush	Kerry
15.	Nader	Nader	Kerry	Bush
16.	Kerry	Kerry/Nader/Bush		
17.	Kerry/Nader	Kerry/Nader	Bush	Bush
18.	Nader	Nader	Kerry	Bush
19.	Bush	Bush	Kerry/Nader	Kerry/Nader

	Strongly Agree	Agree	Disagree	Strongly Disagree
20.	Bush	Bush	Kerry/Nader	Kerry/Nader
21.	Kerry	Kerry	Nader	Bush
22.	Bush	Bush	Nader/Kerry	Nader/Kerry
23.	Nader	Kerry	Bush	
24.	Bush	Kerry	Nader	Nader
25.	Bush	Bush	Kerry/Nader	Kerry/Nader
26.	Nader	Nader	Kerry	Bush
27.	Kerry	Kerry	Bush	Nader
28.	Nader	Kerry	Bush	Bush
29.	Bush	Bush	Kerry	Nader
30.	Bush	Kerry	Nader	Nader
31.	Bush	Kerry	Nader	Nader
32.	Kerry	Nader	Bush	

Totals

Bush	Kerry	Nader

"The right of citizens of the United States to vote shall not be denied or abridged by the United States or by any State on account of race, color, or previous condition of servitude."

—Amendment XV, U.S. Constitution, Ratified February 3, 1870

"The right of citizens of the United States to vote shall not be denied or abridged by the United States or by any State on account of sex."

—Amendment XIX, U.S. Constitution, Ratified August 18, 1920

The Bottom Line: Casting Your Vote

You've given the candidates careful consideration: You've read their positions on all the issues, you've heard all the TV ads and campaign rhetoric. You've decided who will get your vote. Now comes the most important part of the process—going to the polls on November 2 and actually casting your vote.

Before you can vote, you need to know where your polling place is (where you go to cast your vote) and you need to register to vote.

Are You Registered?

First things first: Are you registered, and are you eligible to vote? Every state requires that voters must be citizens of the United States as well as citizens of the state in which they are registering to vote. Table 13.1 lists the voting requirements for each of the 50 states and the District of Columbia. Because there is no federal law that dictates voting requirements, each state has its own law specifying who can vote.

If you're unsure whether you are registered to vote, check your state's election Web site listed in Table 13.3 on **page 212**. These state Web sites provide contact information for your local election board or precinct. You can contact these officials to verify your voter registration status and request a new voter registration card if necessary.

Some states may require or ask you to declare a party affiliation when you register. You will always be able to vote a split ticket (that is, vote for the Democratic candidate for president and the Republican candidate for governor or another local office—or vice versa), but you will usually be required to declare a party affiliation when voting in primary elections.

Keep in mind that in many states after you declare a party affiliation you cannot vote in the other party's primary. Some states may allow you to register as an independent, but then you may not be allowed to vote in any party primary. Refer to your state's election Web site to find out more about what declaring party affiliation means for you when voting in primary elections.

Also, many states require you to register prior to the election, so check Table 13.1 for registration deadlines in your state and be sure to register in plenty of time.

How and Where to Register

In most states, you can register to vote at the following state and local government agencies:

✓ County board of elections

✓ Municipal board of elections

✓ County clerk's office

- ✓ State board of elections or secretary of state's office
- ✓ Driver's licensing office or bureau of motor vehicles
- ✓ Public libraries
- ✓ State or local public aid agencies

Many states offer some form of postcard and/or online voter registration form. In addition, you can go to **http://www.fec.gov/votregis/vr.htm** to download the National Mail Voter Registration Form.

This form is published by the Federal Election Commission to enable anyone to register to vote from anywhere in the United States. The form can be used to

- ✓ Conduct voter registration drives, especially at locations where voters gather from many states, such as colleges and universities or conventions.
- ✓ Register people from surrounding states who work, shop, or attend events in a central city.
- ✓ Register yourself no matter where you live.

All states accept the National Form printed from the computer document on regular paper stock, signed by the applicant, and mailed in an envelope with first class postage. Make sure you consult your state election Web site for information on where and when to send the application (see Table 13.3 on **page 212**). The only exceptions are the following:

- ✓ New Hampshire town and city clerks accept this application only as a request for their own mail-in absentee voter registration form.
- ✓ North Dakota does not have voter registration.
- ✓ Wyoming cannot accept this form under state law.

Table 13.1

State Voter Registration Requirements

State	US Citizen	State Resident	Be at least 18 years old
Alabama	x	State, county	Before election
Alaska	x	State, jurisdiction at least 30 days before election	Within 90 days of registering
Arizona	x	State, county at least 29 days before election	Before election
Arkansas	x	x	Before election
California	x	x	Before election
Colorado	x	30 days before election	On or before election day
Connecticut	x	State, town	On or before election day
Delaware	x	x	On or before election day
Dist. of Columbia	x	30 days before election	Before election
Florida	x	State, county	Before election
Georgia	x	State, county	Within 6 months of registering and before election
Hawaii	x	x	Be at least 16 to register, 18 before election
Idaho	x	State, county at least 30 days before election	On or before election day
Illinois	x	State, precinct at least 30 days before election	Before election
Indiana	x	State, precinct at least 30 days before election	On or before election day
Iowa	x	x	Be at least 171/2 to register, 18 to vote
Kansas	x	x	Before election
Kentucky	x	State, county at least 28 days before election	On or before election day
Louisiana	x	State resident at address where you claim homestead exemption	Before election
Maine	x	State, municipality	Before election
Maryland	x	State, county	Before election
Massachusetts	x	x	Before election
Michigan	x	State, township 30 days before election	Before election
Minnesota	x	20 days before election, reside at given address	Before election
Mississippi	x	State, city, county 30 days before election	Before election

Not convicted of a felony (or have rights restored)	Not mentally incomptetent	Deadline for registration
x	x	10 days before election
x		30 days before election
x	x	October 4, 2004
x	x	30 days before election
x	x	15 days before election
Not confined as a prisoner		29 days before election
x	x	14 days before election
x	x	October 13, 2004
		30 days before election
x	x	30 days before election
x	x	October 4, 2004
x	x	October 4, 2004
x		Election day, or 25 days before by mail
x		27 days before election
Not confined as a prisoner		29 days before election
x	x	10 days before election
x	x	15 days before election
x	x	29 days before election
x	x	30 days before election
		Election day
Not convicted of an "infamous" crime, buying or selling votes, or more than one "crime of violence"	x	20 days before election
Not convicted of a felony or corrupt practices w/ respect to elections	Not be under guardianship w/ respect to voting	20 days before election
Not confined to jail		30 days before election
Not convicted of treason of felony	x	Election day
x	x	30 days before election

State Voter Registration Requirements

State	US Citizen	State Resident	Be at least 18 years old
Missouri	x	x	Before election
Montana	x	State, county 30 days before election	On or before election day
Nebraska	x	x	On or before election day
Nevada	x	State, county, and precinct 10 days before election	On or before election day
New Hampshire	x	x	On or before election day
New Jersey	x	State, county 30 days before election	Before election
New Mexico	x	x	Before election
New York	x	State, county 30 days before election	To register and before election day
North Carolina	x	State, county 30 days before election	Before election
North Dakota			
Ohio	x	x	On or before election day
Oklahoma	x	x	On or before election day
Oregon	x	x	Before election
Pennsylvania	At least 1 month before election	State, election district 30 days before election	On or before election day
Rhode Island	x	State 30 days before election	Before election
South Carolina	x	x	On or before election day
South Dakota	x	x	Before election
Tennessee	x		On or before election day
Texas	x	State, county	Before election
Utah	x	State 30 days before election	On or before election day
Vermont	x	x	On or before election day
Virginia	x	State, precinct	Before election
Washington	x	State, county, precinct 30 days before election	Before election
West Virginia	x	Live at address listed on voter registration	Before election
Wisconsin	x	State 10 days before election	Before election
Wyoming	x	x	On or before election day

Not convicted of a felony (or have rights restored)	Not mentally incomptetent	Deadline for registration
x	x	October 6, 2004
x	x	October 4, 2004
x	x	10 days before election
x	x	October 12, 2004
x		October 23, 2004 or on election day
Not serving a sentence, on parole, or on probation		October 4, 2004
x	x	28 days before election
x	x	Postmark Oct. 8 by mail, Oct. 22 in person
x		25 days before election
		North Dakota does not have voter registration
x	x	October 4, 2004
x	x	25 days before election
		Postmark 21 days election before
		30 days before election
x	x	30 days before election
Not confined to jail, or committed a felony	x	October 2, 2004
x	x	15 days before election
x	x	October 3, 2004
x	x	October 4, 2004
x	x	postmark 20 days before election, in person 8 days before election
		October 25, 2004
x	x	October 4, 2004
x		October 2, 2004, except for in-person at auditor's office: October 18, 2004
x	x	October 13, 2004
x	x	Election day
x	x	October 4, 2004

Note: Polling times vary by location. Check with your local precinct or polling place.

New Voter ID Requirements

In the 2000 presidential election, only 11 states required voters to show a photo ID when voting. Now lawmakers in 25 states have introduced laws requiring voters to produce a valid photo ID to register and/or vote. Some Democrats say the requirement takes away voting rights from citizens who are unlikely to carry ID, such as immigrants and the homeless, whereas some Republicans maintain that this check is the only way to avoid voter fraud.

Whatever your opinion on this matter, be aware that you may be required to show ID in your state when you vote (or register to vote), which could be a change from the last time you registered or voted. Check Table 13.2 for voter ID requirements, and check your state election Web site listed in Table 13.3 on **page 212** for detailed information on valid required ID.

Table 13.2

State	Election Day Holiday	Schools Closed	State Employees Off	Private Employees Off	Voter ID Required
Alabama	No	No	No	No	No
Alaska	No	No	Yes	As needed	Yes
Arizona	No	No	No	No	No
Arkansas	No	No	Yes	3 hrs.	Yes
California	No	No	Max 2 hrs.	Max 2 hrs.	No
Colorado	No	No	Max 2 hrs.	Max 2 hrs.	No
Connecticut	No	Option*	No	No	Yes
Delaware	Yes	Yes	Holiday	No	Yes
District of Columbia	No	No	No	No	No
Florida	No	No	Yes	No	Yes
Georgia	No	No	No	Max 2 hrs.	Yes
Hawaii	Yes	Yes	Holiday	Max 2 hrs.	Yes
Idaho	No	No	No	No	No
Illinois	No	Yes	Holiday	Max 2 hrs.	No
Indiana	Yes	No	Holiday	No	No
Iowa	No	No	Max 3 hrs.	Max 3 hrs.	May
Kansas	No	No	Yes	Max 2 hrs.	No
Kentucky	No	No	4 hrs.	4 hrs.	Yes
Louisiana	Yes	No	Holiday	No	Yes
Maine	No	No	No	No	No

State	Election Day Holiday	Schools Closed	State Employees Off	Private Employees Off	Voter ID Required
Maryland	Yes	5 counties may*	Yes	Max 2 hrs.	No
Massachusetts	No	No	No	No	May
Michigan	No	No	No	No	No
Minnesota	No	No	Yes	Forenoon	May
Mississippi	No	No	No	No	No
Missouri	No	No	No	Max 3 hrs.	Yes
Montana	Yes	No	Holiday	No	No
Nebraska	No	No	No	Max 2 hrs.	No
Nevada	No	No	Max 3 hrs.	Max 3 hrs.	No
New Hampshire	No	No	No	No	No
New Jersey	No	No	Yes	No	No
New Mexico	No	No	Yes	Max 2 hrs.	No
New York	Yes	No	Holiday	Max 2 hrs.	No
North Carolina	No	No	No	No	No
North Dakota	No	No	Yes	No	No
Ohio	Yes	No	No	No	No
Oklahoma	No	No	Yes	Max 2 hrs.	May
Oregon	No	No	Yes	Yes	No
Pennsylvania	No	No	No	No	No
Rhode Island	Yes	Yes	Holiday	No	No
South Carolina	Yes	Yes	Holiday	No	Yes
South Dakota	No	No	Max 2 hrs.	Max 2 hrs.	No
Tennessee	No	No	Max 3 hrs.	Max 3 hrs.	Yes
Texas	Yes	No	Max 2 hrs.	Max 2 hrs.	May
Utah	No	No	Yes	Max 2 hrs.	May
Vermont	No	No	No	No	No
Virginia	No	60% Yes*	No	No	Yes
Washington	No	No	No	No	No
West Virginia	Yes	Yes	Holiday	Max 3 hrs.	Yes
Wisconsin	No	No	No	Max 3 hrs.	May
Wyoming	No	No	Max 1 hr.	Max 1 hr	No

***Note:**

Varies by location. Check your state election Web site.
Check state election web site for specifics on voter ID requirements.

Casting Your Vote

After you have registered in your state as a qualified voter, you are eligible to cast your vote on November 2 for president and other congressional, state, and local offices.

Be Prepared

The best way to ensure that your vote will count on November 2 is to prepare beforehand by following these tips:

- ✓ Check with your county, town, or precinct to find out what type of voting machine or ballot you will use. Ask for instructions on how to use the machine or ballot.
- ✓ Ask your election office for a sample ballot so you can familiarize yourself with the ballot's (or machine screen) layout and use. The sample ballot can also help you prepare for election day by deciding who you want to vote for in each race and which ballot initiatives you want to support (if your state includes those). Sample ballots are often available in local newspapers or on the Web as well.
- ✓ Know where your polling place is. Contact your local election office to make sure of the location. Make sure you know where the polling place is if you have moved since the last election. Some states may require you to re-register if you have moved, so check your state's election Web site to make sure.
- ✓ To avoid lines at your polling place, vote in mid-morning or mid-afternoon, if possible.
- ✓ Check Table 13.3 to see whether your state has a law allowing for time off of work to vote.
- ✓ If asked, cooperate with pollsters conducting exit polls. Letting these pollsters know who you voted for (it should always be anonymous) can help influence others who vote later in the day by giving your candidate support in the polls.
- ✓ Be aware that campaign workers may be allowed to hand out literature at your polling place. Be prepared for them to approach you and do not be intimidated by any campaign workers. If you feel you have been harassed or intimidated by a campaign worker in any way, report the incident to the polling place workers.

- ✓ When you are at the polling place and ready to vote, don't hurry. Ask for voting instructions posted at your polling place, and don't hesitate to ask the poll workers questions. Poll workers can help by explaining how the voting machines work and can assist you as you cast your vote.
- ✓ Bring a valid photo ID to the polling place along with your voter registration card. These will provide proof positive that you are eligible to vote.
- ✓ If your name does not appear on the official voter list at the polling place, check to make sure that you are at the right polling place. If you are at the right polling place, you may ask to cast a provisional ballot. This enables you to cast your vote and then follow up with your local election board to see whether you can prove that you were eligible to vote and were somehow omitted from the voter rolls.
- ✓ If you require assistance in voting, notify the poll worker as you verify your ID. You should be allowed to bring another person to the voting machine with you to help you read the ballot and cast your vote (as long as that person is not a candidate for office).
- ✓ If you encounter problems with the voting machine or ballot, go to a poll worker immediately to inform them of the problem. You should be given a new ballot to place your vote.
- ✓ If you feel your vote was misread or was not properly recorded, be aware that you can file a grievance with your local election office or the Secretary of State.

LAUGH TRACK

"If there's one thing we learned from our last presidential election, it's that democracy is far too important to rely on an outdated, error-prone system like punchcard ballots. So, as we gear up for the 2004 vote, many communities have moved on to electronic voting—a far more high-tech, error-prone system."

—John Stewart

MY VOTE CRASHED

As a response to the problems encountered in Florida and other states in the 2000 presidential election, Congress passed the Help America Vote Act (HAVA) of 2002. HAVA includes guidelines and funding to help local election boards convert from paper or other mechanical voting systems to computerized voting systems.

There have already been a number of problems with computerized voting machines in 2002 and in this year's primaries. The problems include votes that were counted for the wrong candidate as well as votes that were not counted at all. Some voting machines have "crashed" while voters were casting their votes.

One of the chief concerns about the new voting technology is the lack of a paper trail that can be used for recounts. Try to determine what type of voting machine your polling place will use on November 2 and get familiar with the equipment's screen and ballot beforehand if at all possible.

If you feel your vote has been compromised by a computer glitch in any way, notify the polling place workers immediately and be prepared to file a complaint with your local election office or Secretary of State.

Steve Breen—Copley News Service

Know Your Rights

Each state has an election Web site that provides voters with detailed information about voter registration, where to find your polling place, absentee balloting, and what to do if you have recently moved.

Many of these state sites also include a voter's bill of rights, which typically includes the following rights, in compliance with the Help America Vote Act (HAVA) of 2002:

As a registered voter, you have the right to

- ✓ Cast your ballot free from interference in a private and secret manner unless assistance is requested.
- ✓ View written instructions on how to obtain a ballot for voting, how to vote, and how to prepare the ballot for deposit in the ballot box.
- ✓ Ask for and receive further instructions from election judges concerning the manner of voting.
- ✓ View a sample ballot in the polling place before voting.
- ✓ Cast a vote if you are in line before the polls are closed.
- ✓ Ask to have the election judges or person of your choice assist you in voting if you cannot read, are blind, or have any other physical disability and cannot cast your ballot; request curbside voting or a more accessible polling location if needed.
- ✓ Receive another ballot if your ballot is accidentally spoiled or you make an error.
- ✓ Vote on statewide candidates and issues and federal candidates by provisional ballot if the election judges or the election authority cannot determine your registration status.
- ✓ Vote by absentee ballot when permitted by law.
- ✓ File a grievance with the Secretary of State's office if your rights under the Help America Vote Act, Title III, have been violated.

Be aware of these rights when you cast your vote. If you have any concerns that your rights as a voter have been violated, do not hesitate to file a grievance with the appropriate election official.

Table 13.3 State Election Web Sites

State	Web Site
Alabama	http://www.sos.state.al.us/election/general/voterid2003.cfm
Alaska	http://www.gov.state.ak.us/ltgov/elections/homepage.html
Arizona	http://www.sos.state.az.us/election/voterregistration.htm
Arkansas	http://www.sosweb.state.ar.us/elections.html
California	http://www.ss.ca.gov/elections/elections_vr.htm
Colorado	http://www.sos.state.co.us/pubs/elections/main.htm
Connecticut	http://www.sots.state.ct.us/ElectionsDivision/ElectionIndex.html
Delaware	http://www.state.de.us/election/voter_services.html
District of Columbia	http://www.dcboee.org/serv/voter_registration.shtm
Florida	http://election.dos.state.fl.us/index.html
Georgia	http://www.sos.state.ga.us/elections/voter_registration/default.htm
Hawaii	http://www.hawaii.gov/elections/voterreg.html
Idaho	http://www.idsos.state.id.us/elect/voterreg/vtr_reg.htm
Illinois	http://www.elections.state.il.us/VoteInfo/pages/Register.htm
Indiana	http://www.in.gov/sos/elections/voters/
Iowa	http://www.sos.state.ia.us/elections/voterreg/
Kansas	http://www.kssos.org/elections/elections_registration.html
Kentucky	http://www.kysos.com/Elecfil/register/reginstruction.asp
Louisiana	http://www.sec.state.la.us/elections/elections-index.htm
Maine	http://www.maine.gov/sos/cec/elec/votreg.htm
Maryland	http://www.elections.state.md.us/citizens/how_to_vote.html

State	Web Site
Massachusetts	http://www.state.ma.us/sec/ele/eleifv/howreg.htm
Michigan	http://www.michigan.gov/sos/ 0,1607,7-127-1633_8716_8726-21727—,00.html
Minnesota	http://www.sos.state.mn.us/election/register.html
Mississippi	http://www.sos.state.ms.us/elections/elections.asp
Missouri	http://www.sos.mo.gov/section4.asp
Montana	http://sos.state.mt.us/css/ELB/Voter_Information.asp# How%20to%20Register%20to%20Vote
Nebraska	http://www.sos.state.ne.us/Elections/voteregpage.htm
Nevada	http://sos.state.nv.us/nvelection/faq.htm#regis
New Hampshire	http://www.sos.nh.gov/voting%20in%20new%20 hampshire%20new.htm
New Jersey	http://www.state.nj.us/lps/elections/electionshome.html
New Mexico	http://www.sos.state.nm.us/Election/ElectionInfo.htm
New York	http://www.elections.state.ny.us/voting/voting.htm
North Carolina	http://www.sboe.state.nc.us/
North Dakota	http://www.state.nd.us/sec/electvote/
Ohio	http://www.sos.state.oh.us/sos//elections/index.html
Oklahoma	http://www.elections.state.ok.us/voterreg.html
Oregon	http://www.sos.state.or.us/elections/votreg/vreg.htm
Pennsylvania	http://www.dos.state.pa.us/voting/
Rhode Island	http://www2.corps.state.ri.us/ELECTIONS/elections_division.htm
South Carolina	http://www.state.sc.us/scsec/
South Dakota	http://www.sdsos.gov/elections/

Table 13.3 Continued

State	Web Site
Tennessee	**http://www.state.tn.us/sos/election.htm**
Texas	**http://www.sos.state.tx.us/elections/index.shtml**
Utah	**http://www.elections.utah.gov/**
Vermont	**http://vermont-elections.org/soshome.htm**
Virginia	**http://www.sbe.state.va.us/**
Washington	**http://www.secstate.wa.gov/elections/**
West Virginia	**http://www.wvsos.com/elections/voters/registernow.htm**
Wisconsin	**http://elections.state.wi.us/**
Wyoming	**http://soswy.state.wy.us/election/reg.htm**

Index

NUMBERS

A

B

C

F

G – H

L – M

N

O – P

Q – R

S – T

U – V

W – X – Y – Z